THE
TOYMAKER

THE TOYMAKER

Andrew Calder

With illustrations by the author

McGraw-Hill Book Company

*New York St. Louis San Francisco Toronto
Dusseldorf Mexico*

First published 1975 by Wolfe Publishing Limited
10 Earlham Street, London WC2H 9LP

© Wolfe Publishing Limited, 1975

123456789   M U B P   79876

Library of Congress Cataloging in Publication Data

Calder, Andrew.
The toymaker.

1. Wooden toy making.   I. Title.
TT174.5.W6C34   1976   745.59'2   75-30694
ISBN 0-07-009604-X

Published and distributed in the United States by McGraw-Hill,
1976

CONTENTS

Introduction

To make the toys described and illustrated in this book, no special skills or expensive tools or materials are necessary. If you are capable of sawing in a straight line and to a given shape, keeping edges and corners square, you will have no difficulty in making these sturdy and attractive toys which will bring many hours of delight to any child. To obtain the best results, however, a few basic points should be borne in mind.

How to use the grids

Use the grids marked on some of the illustrations to obtain full size plans. The grids on the diagrams represent 2 in. squares. Draw your own grid of 2 in. squares on a sheet of paper and transfer the shape by marking with dots on your own grid each point where the lines of the shape illustrated cross the lines of the grid in the diagram. Join up the dots, taking care to follow the shape of any curves. Transfer the full size plan to your material.

English and metric sizes

Timber and board are now sold in metric sizes, as are other materials for do-it-yourself work. For the most part, the sizes in which timber and board are sold have hardly changed, and no problems will therefore be encountered in using the instructions given in this book, which are in the more familiar Imperial units.

For the smaller sections of timber and for boards the equivalent metric sizes, which are slightly smaller than the corresponding Imperial ones, are as follows:

Inches	Millimetres
$\frac{3}{4}$	19
1	25
$1\frac{1}{2}$	38
$1\frac{3}{4}$	44
2	50
$2\frac{1}{2}$	63

These are nominal sizes; prepared timber is always a little smaller. Conversion is simple enough; for example, the metric equivalent of 2 in. × 1 in. batten is 50 × 25 mm. *All* sizes mentioned in the text are *finished* sizes.

For lengths it is useful to remember that 1.8 metres is a little less than 6 ft. (5 ft. 11 in. approximately). In working with smaller dimensions, another useful equivalent is that 300 mm. is close to, but slightly less than, a foot.

Using a craft knife

Great care must be taken when cutting with a craft knife. Always use a steel rule or straight edge and baseboard and keep your cutting edge sharp. Blunt tools spoil the finish by crumbling the wood. Cut through the wood gradually with light strokes, particularly when cutting with the grain.

Using a fretsaw or coping saw

The blade must be fitted into the fretsaw or coping saw with its teeth pointed downward; only the downward strokes are used for cutting. The angle of the blade is not adjustable but the blade is fine enough to follow curves and quite intricate shapes without being turned. Do not under any circumstances force the blade so that it bends while cutting, and take great care to keep the blade upright and at 90° to the surface of the plywood all the time. It is easier to use a fretsaw or coping saw if you are sitting down and holding the work at chest level. Do not try to cut too large a piece of plywood at a time or you will find difficulty in manipulating the saw frame round the edges of the wood.

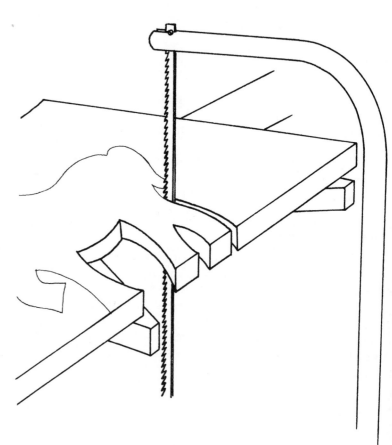

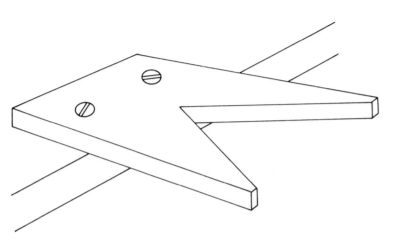

to become tacky before they are brought together. 'G' clamps can be used to hold the parts in contact until the glue has set. (The manufacturer's instructions will indicate the time required.) If 'G' clamps are not available, a pile of old books or other heavy objects can be used instead.

For gluing larger areas, as in the scooter, one of the adhesives specially made for woodwork, such as Evo-stik W, can be used. The purpose of gluing is to further strengthen nailed or screwed sections.

Sawing awkward shapes

This type of operation is greatly simplified if a sawing block is used. This is easily made from an odd piece of plywood about 6 in. × 4 in., with a 'V' section removed from one end. When screwed or clamped to a work bench, it will be found an excellent base.

Cutting out shapes

Continually check that all edges are square and all right angles accurate, or you will have difficulty in assembling the toys.

Glues

Where glue is needed in assembling the smaller toys any multipurpose adhesive such as Bostik, UHU, or Croid will serve. It should be spread thinly on both surfaces and allowed

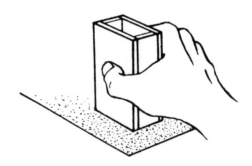

Sanding

When sanding wood smooth in preparation for painting or varnishing, you may find it useful to glue pieces of fine sandpaper to a flat piece of board. Gently and smoothly rub the surface to be sanded against the prepared board, taking care not to round off any edges or corners. Care must be taken to avoid splintering or tearing the grain by rubbing too hard or using too coarse a sandpaper. Always work *with* the grain. Sanding across the grain produces scratches which take a long time to remove and which show up even more beneath varnish or paint.

When sanding awkwardly shaped pieces, glue strips of sandpaper to small pieces of card to make files.

Painting

When painting small toys for younger children, remember to use non-toxic paints.

Safety

If they are made as described, the toys in this book will be perfectly safe. Where the weight of one or more children has to be borne it is vital that the appropriate sizes of timber and board (as indicated in the text) should be used and that all joints should be made as recommended; any skimping or over-hasty work here could have serious results.

Remember that the basic instructions are for toddlers' toys: the climbing frame, swing and slide and the wheeled toys are not intended for use by larger children. Information is given in the text on using thicker timber and adjusting dimensions where heavier use is expected, but toys of this kind can hardly be made proof against the determined assaults of, say, a ten-year-old.

Once in use, such toys should be looked over at frequent intervals (say, once a week) to make sure that they are secure. Joints and suspension cords should be given particular attention. Wheels, axles and steering are other obvious items to check. A watch should also be kept for any signs of splintering, which should be dealt with immediately.

Where the smaller toys are concerned, the most important thing is to be sure that the initial construction is sound: a broken toy can be dangerous. It is worth taking a lot of trouble to make sure that all surfaces that could possibly be reached by a child's fingers are sanded smooth before painting or varnishing. The paints themselves *must* be non-toxic; do not be tempted to use other types, even if the shops have just closed and you are desperately anxious to finish the job – it simply isn't worth the risk.

THE ARRANGEMENT OF THIS BOOK

In the following pages the smaller toys, all of which are models of one kind or another and are essentially for indoor use, are described first: string puppets, ninepin soldiers and cannon, the play lorry or play truck, Noah's ark and animals, the pull-along snake and alligator, and farmyard. These are also among the simplest of the toys to make.

The remaining toys, beginning with the play tunnel, are larger and can be used out of doors. For the most part, they provide for adventure as well as for imaginative play. They are arranged roughly in order of complexity, but if the instructions are followed carefully there should be no difficulty in building any of them.

String puppets

The following instructions are for a clown (Fig. 1) and a witch (Fig. 13) but, with very slight modification, the basic constructions can be used to create whatever characters you wish.

TOOLS

Tenon saw
Brace and bit, or drill
Craft knife, such as a Stanley 199 with normal duty blades No. 1991
Pair of pliers
Piece of hardboard or plywood as a cutting board
Two small soft paintbrushes, one from a child's paintbox or artists' suppliers for face detail

The clown

MATERIALS

The body of the puppet is a $2\frac{3}{4}$ in. length of 2 in. $\times \frac{7}{8}$ in. (or 2 in. $\times$ 1 in.) softwood. The head is a $2\frac{1}{4}$ in. diameter ball of wood, polystyrene or plastic, with a $\frac{3}{4}$ in. diameter ball for the nose. The limbs are made from a couple of lengths of $\frac{1}{4}$ in. to $\frac{3}{8}$ in.

Fig. 1. The clown

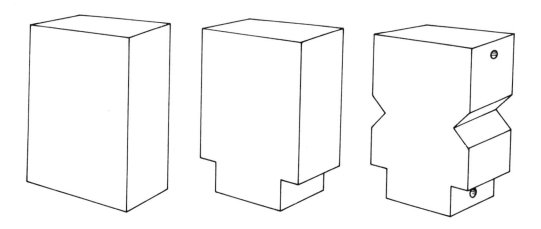

Fig. 2. Puppet body

garden cane, jointed with four $\frac{1}{2}$ in. diameter wood or plastic beads. The hands are made from a piece of $\frac{1}{8}$ in. thick card, hardboard or wood about 3 in. × 2 in. and the feet from an 8 in. length of 1 in. × $\frac{5}{8}$ in. wood. The manipulating frame is made from two pieces of thin wood 4 in. × 3 in.

In addition you will need 'Terylene' or nylon thread of the same thickness as kite string, clear adhesive, paint, scraps of fur fabric or rug wool for hair and, to make the clothes, scraps of fabric or felt, a needle and thread and two large buttons.

METHOD

The body (Fig. 2) is cut from the length of 2 in. × $\frac{7}{8}$ in. (or 2 in. × 1 in.) wood with the waist and leg recesses removed as shown in Fig. 2. The waist notches are not really necessary for this clown, for his baggy trousers are held up by straps, but this

shape is shown so that the puppet's body can be adapted for other characters.

Drill the holes right through the body from side to side to support arms and legs (Fig. 3) or, if you prefer, screw small eye hooks into place. Should you wish to give the puppet sideways movement from the waist to enable it to twist round without moving its feet from the stage, then make the body from a 2 in. diameter circle cut from wood 1 in. thick or several thicknesses of plywood glued together. Cut the circle in half and invert the two halves, joining them together with a hook and staple or two staples (Fig. 4).

The head is made from the $2\frac{1}{4}$ in. diameter wooden ball with the smaller ball glued on as a nose. The head and face detail must be painted before gluing the hair. Rug wool or ordinary knitting wool will do admirably for hair or, if you prefer, a strip of fur fabric may be glued round the head to leave a bald patch.

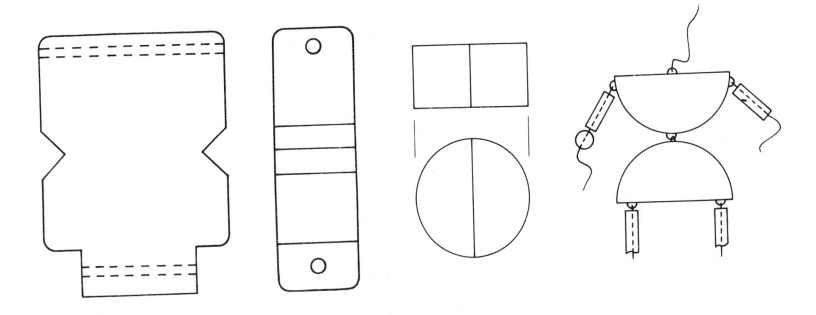

Fig. 3. Holes for arms and legs

Fig. 4. Body with sideways movement

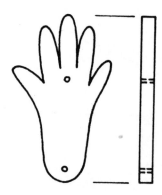

Fig. 5. Hands

Fig. 6. Feet

16

You can, of course, glue the strip around the front of the head under the nose to make a bushy beard which, with the bald head, makes a super clown. Why not make both?

The arms and legs are made from short sections of cane tubing with wooden beads as the joints. To make this tubing, cut the cane between the 'knuckles' into four sections $1\frac{1}{8}$ in. long and four sections $1\frac{1}{2}$ in. long. The soft centre is easily cleaned out with a piece of wire.

Trace the hands from Fig. 5, and transfer the outlines to a piece of $\frac{1}{8}$ in. card, hardboard or wood. Cut out with the craft knife. The two holes are easily made with a large needle or drilled with a small bit. Sand smooth and paint white.

The feet are two 4 in. lengths of 1 in. $\times \frac{5}{8}$ in. wood shaped with the craft knife to the size and shape shown in the plan and elevations shown in Fig. 6. Drill or bore the two holes, then sand smooth and finish in black gloss paint.

The clown is now ready to assemble, as shown in Fig. 7. If the head is wooden, it is attached to the body by an eye and staple, or two staples. If it is of polystyrene or plastic, a piece of wire can be pushed through the head to protrude at top and bottom. The ends can then be looped with the pliers to form, at the top, a ring to suspend the puppet by and, at the bottom, a ring with which to attach the head to the body.

Tie one hand to a 10 in. length of thread and pass the other end through a short section of cane, a bead, then another short section of cane. The thread is then passed through the body armhole and a further two short pieces of cane and a bead are threaded on before tying the other hand. Make sure that the arm sections are not pulled too tight and that there is plenty of flopping movement. Trim off the loose ends of thread and, using the longer pieces of cane and the remaining beads, repeat the procedure for the legs.

The clown is now ready for his clothes, which are easily made

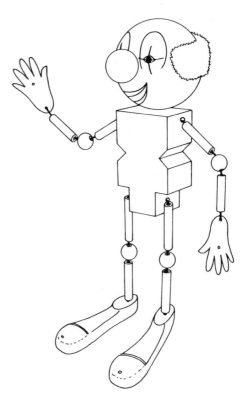

Fig. 7. Clown: complete body

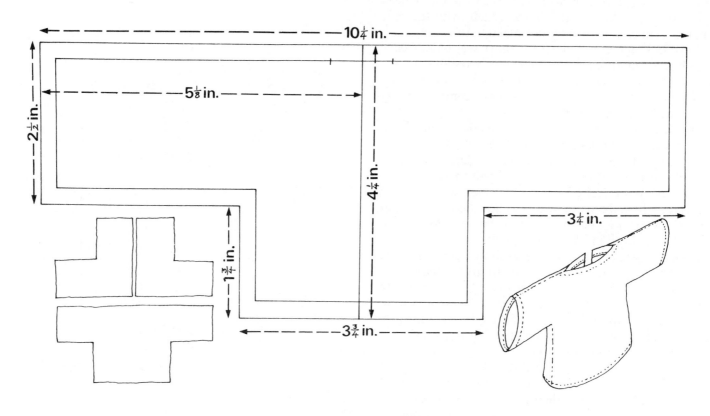

Fig. 8. Shirt for clown.

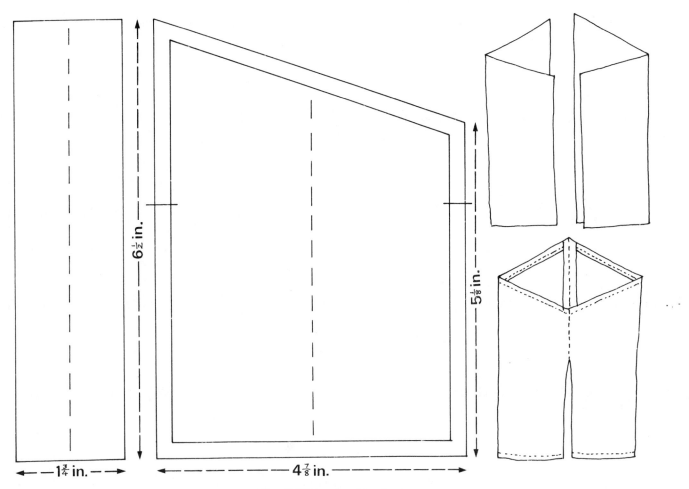

Fig. 9. Trousers for clown.

$1\frac{3}{4}$ in.

$6\frac{1}{2}$ in.

$4\frac{7}{8}$ in.

$5\frac{1}{8}$ in.

19

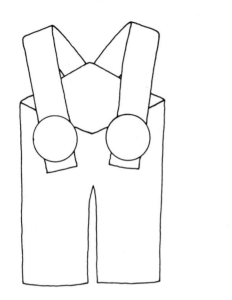 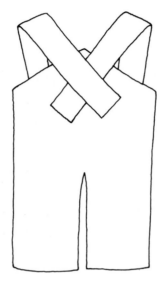 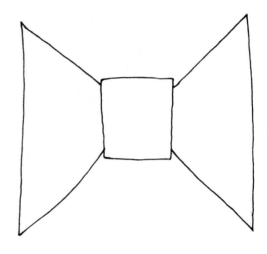

Fig. 10. Straps for clown

Fig. 11. Bow

from scraps of fabric or felt.

Cut two pieces of fabric for the shirt, halving one of them down the middle as shown. The two pieces are then sewn together and hemmed. The inner line shows the hems. The trousers are shown in Fig. 9. They consist simply of two pieces of material folded over and sewn together as shown. The straps are two pieces of fabric, folded over and sewn and then stitched to the trousers as shown in Fig. 10. The two large buttons are then fixed to the front of the straps. The bow tie can be made from an actual bow, or cut from card to the shape shown in Fig. 11 with fabric glued to it. The clown can now be dressed and his bow tie stitched or glued on.

To work the puppet, glue or nail together two thin pieces of wood about 4 in. × $\frac{3}{4}$ in. (Fig. 12). For a small child, a simpler puppet can be made controlled with only one piece. Attach a length of thread to the back of the body through the shirt, or to the top of the head as the main support, and fix it to the centre of the frame. The hands and feet are fixed to the ends of the frame. A little trial and error is necessary to get the length of the strings correct. They should all hang level when the puppet is suspended in the air. When it is touching the ground, make sure that the frame is at a comfortable height for you to control. Further strings can be added to give more movement. If, for example, the puppet is suspended by the body, strings on both sides of the head will enable the head to be turned or to waggle from side to side.

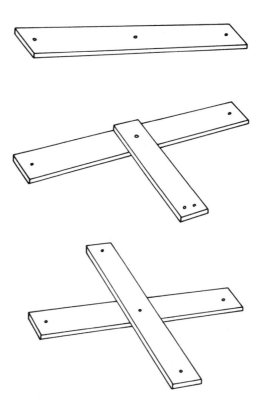

Fig. 12. Controls for puppets

The witch

MATERIALS

The witch (Fig. 13) is simply made using modelling clay and thick string. As for the clown, you will need in addition nylon thread, clear adhesive, paint, rug or nylon wool, scraps of fabric and a needle and thread. You will also require an eye screw and some embroidery silk.

A piece of string 11 in. long is knotted at each extreme end. Another 9½ in. length is knotted at each end, and around the first piece about 1 in. from the knot at one end to form arms, as shown in Fig. 14.

METHOD

Mould a piece of clay round the head knot and model the nose and features. Although the witch has no ears, you may wish to add these for other characters. A larger lump of clay is needed for the chest and another for the abdomen. The arms and legs are made from small lumps of clay moulded round the limb strings, the feet and hands being formed round the knots.

Before the clay hardens, pierce a hole through each hand and foot, and fix an eye screw or wire loop to the head to attach the threads.

When the clay has hardened, the eyes and wrinkles can be painted on to the head and the hair glued on. Nylon wool can be used for hair. The feet can be painted with black gloss paint. The witch is then ready for her clothing.

The dress is a longer version of the clown's shirt, Fig. 16. The cloak and hood are traced from Fig.17, and should be hemmed

Fig. 13. The witch

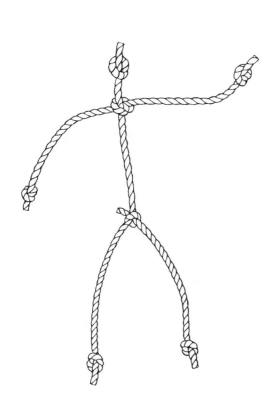

Fig. 14. String skeleton for witch

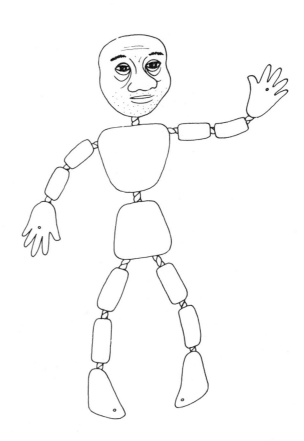

Fig. 15. Clay body added to skeleton

23

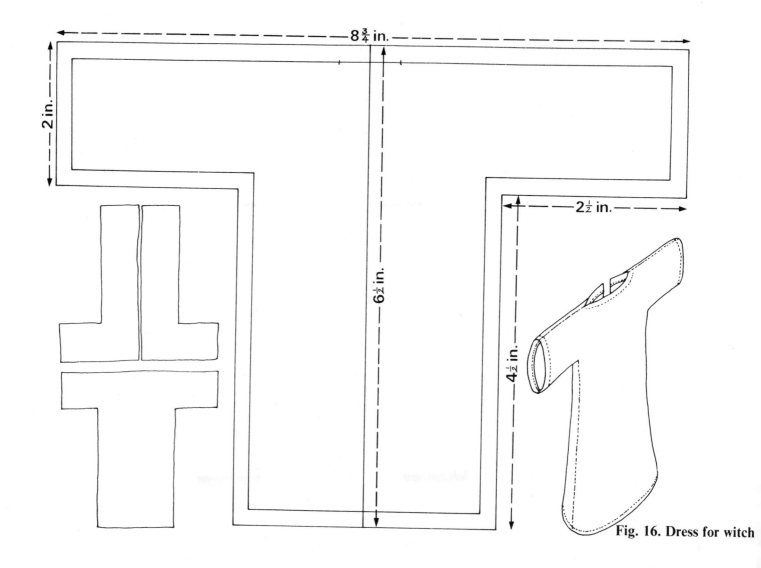

Fig. 16. Dress for witch

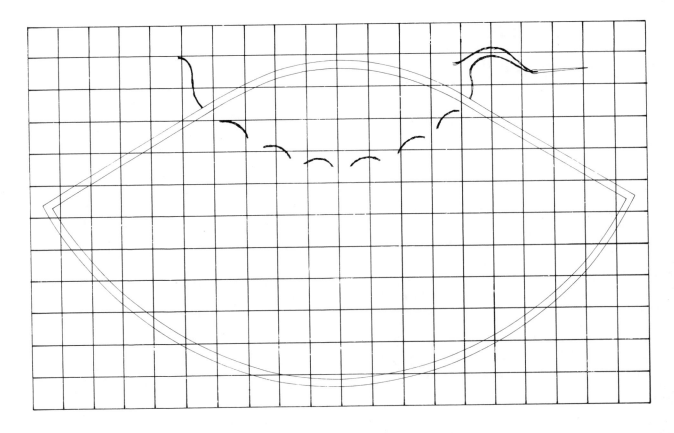

Fig. 17. Cloak for witch. Grid shows 1 in. squares

all round.   The hood is formed by making large stitches with embroidery silk as shown and drawing the ends tight round the puppet's neck, tying the ends in a bow.

The frame and threads for manipulating the witch are made in exactly the same way as for the clown.

Using the methods described above you will find it easy to make a whole collection of puppets. Even animals can be made using the same basic skeletons.

Ninepin soldiers and cannon set

TOOLS

Tenon saw
Fretsaw or coping saw
Hammer
Sandpaper
Several small paintbrushes
   (from a child's paintbox or artists' suppliers)

MATERIALS

The ninepin soldiers (Fig. 1) are made entirely from lengths of wooden dowel glued together, with the exception of the hat decorations which are made from $1\frac{1}{4}$ in. lengths of Popsicle stick. The cannon is made entirely from plywood $\frac{3}{16}$ in. or $\frac{1}{4}$ in. thick, glued and pinned together. The cannon balls are $1\frac{1}{2}$ in. diameter wooden balls. You will also require a general-purpose clear adhesive.

The ninepins

METHOD

The ninepins are made from several lengths of wooden dowel simply glued together. The body is a $2\frac{5}{8}$ in. length of $\frac{3}{4}$ in.

Fig. 1. Ninepin soldier

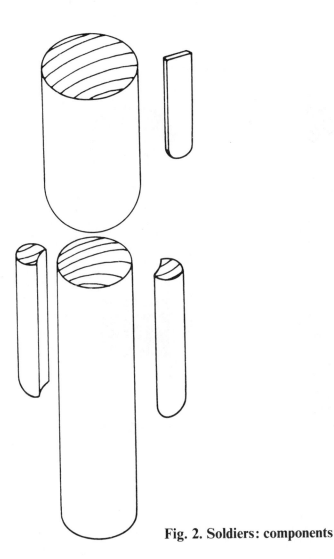

Fig. 2. Soldiers: components

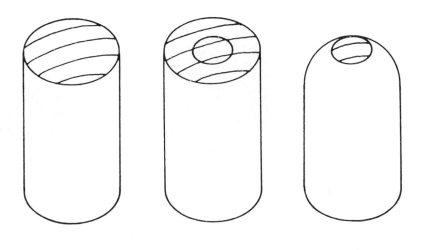

Fig. 3. Shaping the head

diameter dowel with a $1\frac{5}{8}$ in. length of 1 in. diameter dowel for the head and two $1\frac{1}{2}$ in. lengths of $\frac{3}{8}$ in. dowel for the arms. As can be seen from Fig. 2, the head must be shaped at the lower end and the arms shaped to fit the body.

The body is made by simply cutting a $2\frac{5}{8}$ in. length of $\frac{3}{4}$ in. dowel, ensuring that both ends are at right-angles to the sides. Sand smooth and check that the body when placed upright on either end stands firmly and at ninety degrees to the surface on which it is standing.

To make the head, cut a $1\frac{1}{2}$ in. length of 1 in. diameter dowel, making sure that the end surfaces are flat and at right-angles to the sides (Fig. 3). A $\frac{1}{2}$ in. circle is then marked centrally on one end and the end rounded off equally all round, leaving the central circle intact. Sand smooth, making sure that the head

Fig. 4. Soldier, (a) with bearskin, (b) with peaked hat, (c) bareheaded

28

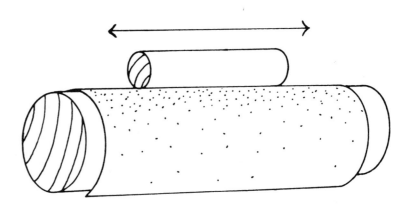

stands squarely upright on the flat surface of the rounded end.

Should you wish the soldiers to wear bearskin headresses, the top end of the head dowel must be rounded off completely (Fig. 4a). A peak may be added to a flat-topped head dowel (Fig. 4b) or a 1 in. diameter wooden ball can be used to make the head of a ninepin without a hat (Fig. 4c).

Cut two 1½ in. lengths of ⅜ in. dowel for the arms. To shape the arms so that they can be glued firmly to the body, first wrap a piece of sandpaper round a length of 1 in. diameter dowel and then, in a lengthwise to and fro motion, sand one side of the arm dowel until a sufficiently wide surface has been shaped for the arm to be glued securely (Fig. 5). The hand must then be shaped by rounding off one end of the arm on the opposite side to the gluing surface.

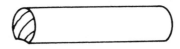

Fig. 5. Shaping the arms

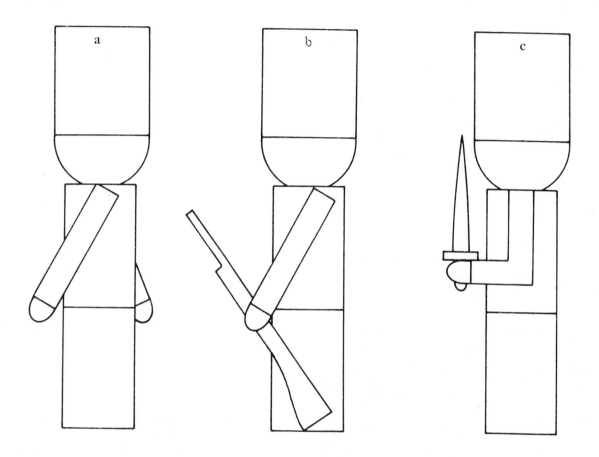

Fig. 6. Variations, including rifles and swords

The head and arms are now glued to the body and allowed to dry. The hat decoration is made by cutting a $1\frac{1}{4}$ in. length of Popsicle stick and gluing it on the upper part of the head dowel as shown in Figs. 1 and 2.

When the adhesive is completely dry the ninepins can be painted to your choice. Any number of soldiers can be made and, if some are made with their arms in various positions and with rifles or swords (cut to the shapes shown in Fig. 6, from card or thin wood), they will make a splendid set of toy soldiers which any small boy would be proud to own.

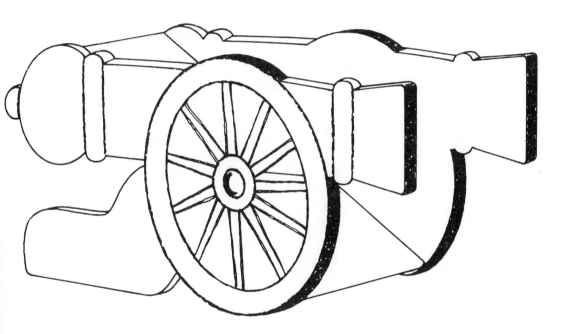

Fig. 7. The cannon

The cannon

Although the cannon (Fig. 7) may at first appear more difficult, it is in fact nothing more than a decorative ramp down which to roll the cannon balls to knock down the ninepins. It is made

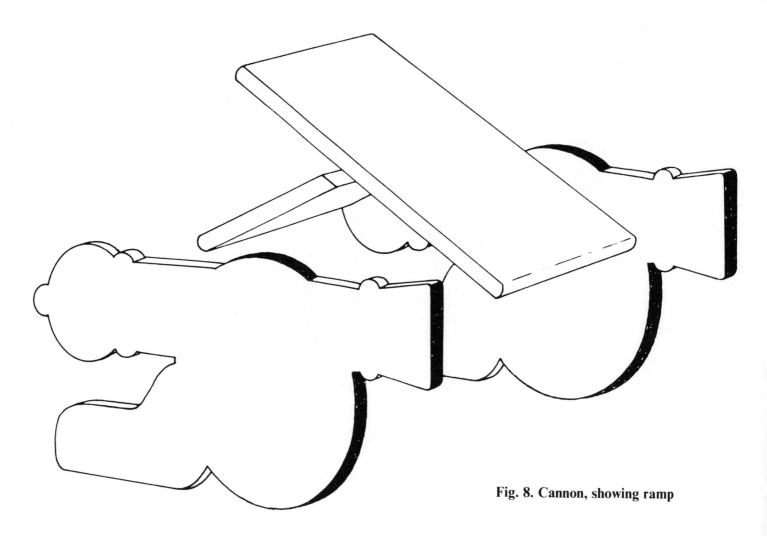

Fig. 8. Cannon, showing ramp

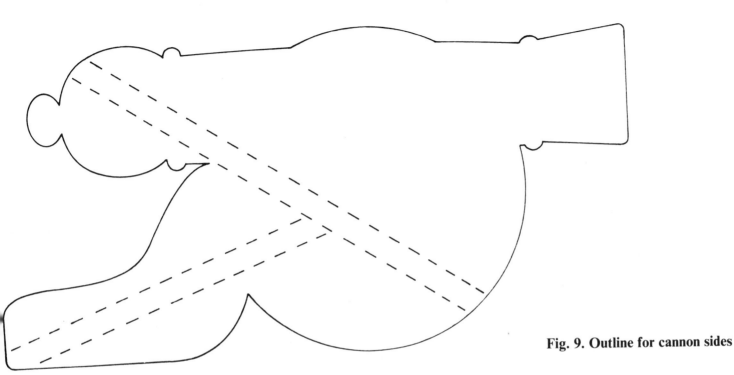

Fig. 9. Outline for cannon sides

from four pieces of plywood: two shaped as a cannon and two forming the actual ramps (Fig. 8). The plywood used can be up to $\frac{1}{4}$ in. thick. Trace Fig. 9 to get the outline of the cannon sides and transfer it to one piece of plywood. Reverse the tracing and transfer the other side on to another piece of plywood.

The two sides of the cannon can now be cut out with the fretsaw or coping saw using the sawing block described on page 9. As the blades of a fretsaw or coping saw are fine there will be no difficulty in sanding the edges smooth. Make sure that both sides of the cannon are identical in size and shape.

The two ramps sections are a 5 in. and a $3\frac{3}{4}$ in. length of $\frac{1}{4}$ in. plywood or timber $1\frac{5}{8}$ in. wide. They are glued and pinned between the two cannon side pieces (see Figs. 8 and 9). It will be found easier to paint the cannon details on the sides before

33

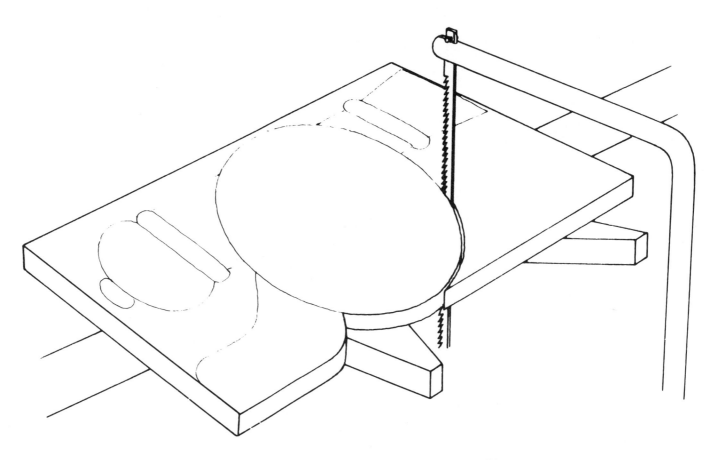

Fig. 10. Cutting out cannon sides

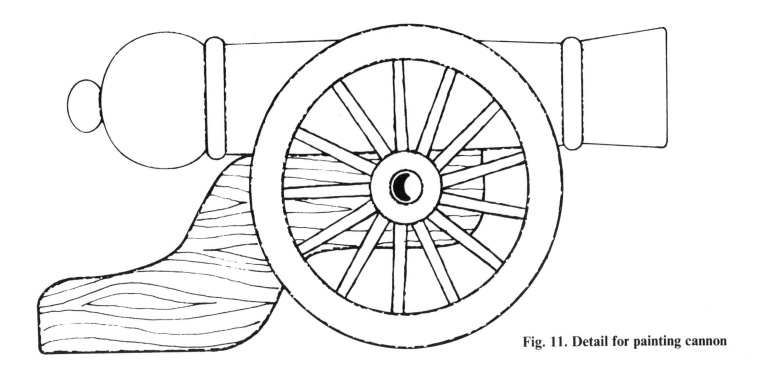

Fig. 11. Detail for painting cannon

assembly. Trace the detail from Fig. 11. The ramp and inner sides can be painted white when the complete unit is assembled. Non-toxic gloss paints can easily be used with the small paintbrushes and there should be no difficulty in painting the sides if the tracings are bold enough. Do not use too much paint. Allow the sides to dry flat and allow one colour to dry before applying another.

The cannon-balls are painted black and allowed to dry. The ninepin soldiers set is now ready. If two sets are made, an excellent battle can be fought in which each of the two sides tries to knock all the opponents' soldiers over first.

35

Play truck

TOOLS

Tenon saw
Fretsaw or coping saw
Brace and bit or drill
Pair of compasses, or jar or tin lid, $2\frac{1}{8}$ in. $\times$ $2\frac{1}{4}$ in. in diameter
Hammer
Sandpaper
Paintbrushes

MATERIALS

The play truck (Fig. 1) is made almost entirely from $\frac{1}{4}$ in. plywood with the exception of the axles, chassis, headlamps and radiator. The axles are two $7\frac{3}{8}$ in. lengths of $\frac{1}{8}$ in. dowel and the chassis is made of two $10\frac{1}{2}$ in. lengths of $\frac{3}{4}$ in. $\times$ $\frac{1}{2}$ in. batten. The wheels can be of $\frac{1}{2}$ in. plywood or can be of two thicknesses of $\frac{1}{4}$ in. plywood glued together. The headlamps are two $\frac{1}{2}$ in. slices of 1 in. dowel and the radiator is cut from $\frac{3}{4}$ in. thick softwood.

METHOD

The truck is made in three parts: (a) the cab, (b) the chassis and wheels, and (c) the load-carrying box or container. The box can be made removable, enabling miniature logs, drums and so on

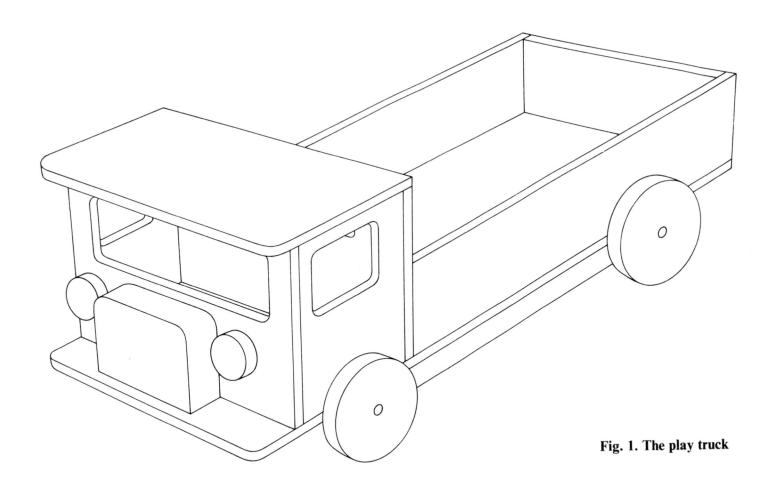

Fig. 1. The play truck

Fig. 2. Parts for cab. Illustration half full-size

to be carried with the positioning bars acting as stops to prevent the load from falling off.

The cab

Use Fig. 2 to cut the cab to the right size and shape.

The illustrations for the cab are shown half full-size. The load box and chassis components are illustrated at one third full-size. To make a larger truck take care to enlarge all the parts proportionately.

Cut out the pieces, checking that all right-angled corners are accurate. To cut out the windows, first drill within the area to be removed a hole large enough easily to accommodate the blade of your fretsaw or coping saw (Fig. 3). Remove the blade from the saw frame and, placing the blade through the drilled hole in the panel, replace the ends in the frame so that the saw and panel are now linked together. The teeth of the saw blade must point downwards when it is fitted in the saw frame. The windows can now be cut out and the blade removed from the saw once again to extricate it from the panel. Repeat this operation for each window. Hints on using a fretsaw are given on p. 8. The cutting of the windows will be simplified by the use of a sawing block, made from a piece of plywood as described on p. 9. Since the blade of a fretsaw or coping saw is fine, there will be no difficulty in sanding the edges smooth. Sand smooth all five pieces, taking care not to round off any edges or corners that are intended to be square. Glue and pin together the parts in the positions shown in Fig. 4.

The radiator is a $1\frac{3}{4}$ in. $\times$ $2\frac{3}{4}$ in. piece of softwood $\frac{3}{4}$ in. thick, with the two upper corners rounded off. The headlamps are two $\frac{1}{2}$ in. slices of 1 in. dowel, cut with the tenon saw and sanded smooth. Sanding will be easier if a sheet of sandpaper is glued to a piece of hardboard or plywood and the surface to be

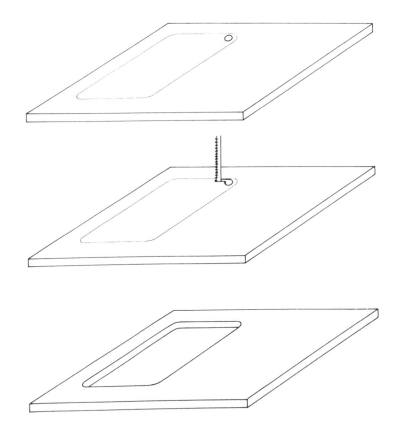

Fig. 3. Method of cutting out cab windows

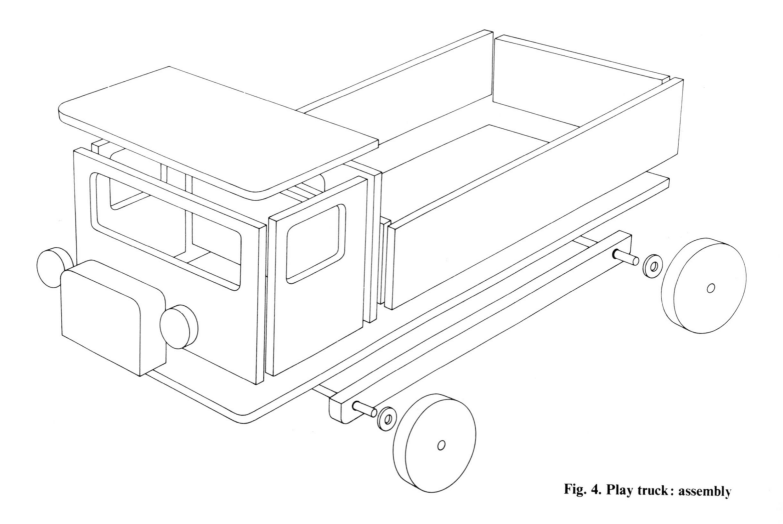

Fig. 4. Play truck: assembly

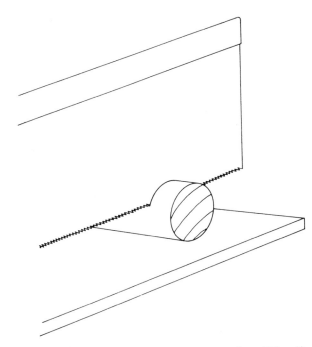

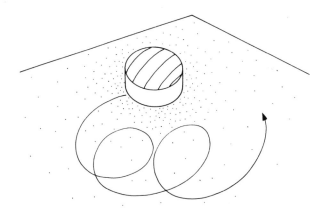

Fig. 5. Cutting and sanding headlamps

sanded is rubbed on it in a circular motion (Fig. 5).

Glue and pin the headlamps and radiator in position as shown in Fig. 4.

The chassis

The chassis comprises the main truck base, the chassis battens, the wheel axles and the wheels. Cut the base from plywood as for the cab, using the plan in Fig. 6, and sand it smooth, taking care to keep the edges square and straight. The two chassis battens are then cut from $\frac{3}{4}$ in. × $\frac{1}{2}$ in. batten and the holes are drilled in each in the positions shown in Fig. 6. The battens are then glued and pinned into position as shown in Fig. 7.

The wheels can be cut from $\frac{1}{2}$ in. plywood or from two thicknesses of $\frac{1}{4}$ in. plywood glued together. Any multi-purpose adhesive will do if spread thinly on both surfaces to be joined and allowed to become tacky before placing them together. A couple of 'G'-clamps with some waste plywood or hardboard to protect the wheel will hold the two thicknesses together while the adhesive is drying. If you have no clamps, anything heavy, such as a pile of old books, will do just as well.

Before cutting out each wheel, drill the axle hole, making absolutely sure that the hole is central. It should be small enough for the axle dowel to be a really tight fit. Using the sawing block, carefully cut out the wheels with the fretsaw or

Fig. 6.
Load box and chassis components
shown one third full-size

42

coping saw (see p. 8). Extreme care must be taken to ensure that the wheels are perfectly circular. Sand smooth and paint or varnish the wheel and chassis battens before inserting the axles through the battens and into the wheels.

Before the wheels are fixed to the axles, a metal or plastic washer must be placed between the chassis batten and each wheel as shown in Fig. 7 to ensure that the wheel will turn smoothly without rubbing against the truck sides. If the ends of the axles are lightly smeared with adhesive and the axles are a tight fit in the wheels, it is extremely unlikely that the wheels will fall off. Should a wheel become loose at any time, a wedge can be inserted into the end of the axles, or an upholstery tack

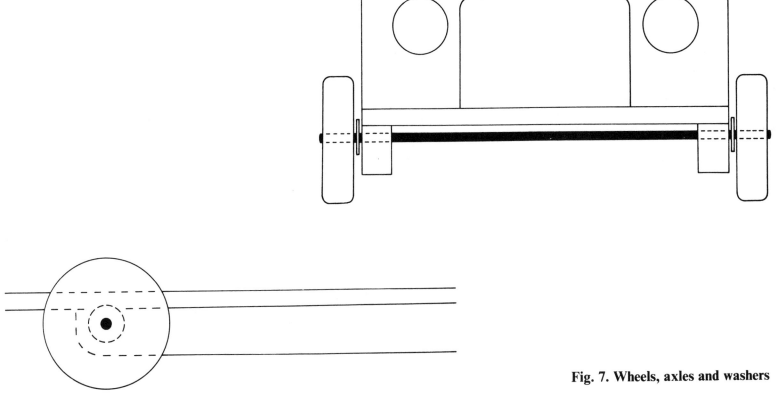

Fig. 7. Wheels, axles and washers

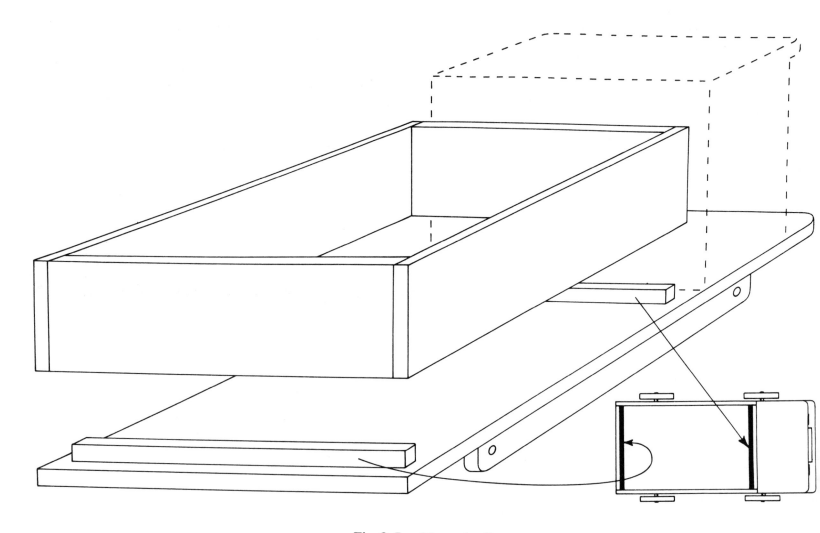

Fig. 8. Load box: details

can be pushed in centrally and can double as a hub cap.

The load box or container

Cut the four rectangular pieces shown in Fig. 6, taking great care to keep all edges and corners square. Sand these smooth and glue and pin them together as shown in Fig. 8. The box structure can be left loose to slot over two $5\frac{7}{16}$ in. lengths of batten fixed to the main truck base, or it can be fixed permanently to the base and driver's cab when the whole truck is assembled.

Assembly and finishing

The truck can now be assembled as shown in Fig. 1 and sanded. When sanding smooth, particularly the larger flat surfaces, always work *with* the grain (see p. 9).

The truck can now be varnished or gaily painted to your choice. Thin the first coat sufficiently to seal the surface of the plywood.

Noah's ark and animals

TOOLS

Tenon saw
Fretsaw or coping saw
Brace and bit or drill
Hammer
Sandpaper
Paintbrush
Try square or set square

The Ark

MATERIALS

The ark is made entirely from $\frac{1}{4}$ in. plywood, with the exception of the roof slopes, which can be of hardboard. When varnished, this contrasts beautifully with the plywood. Alternatively, $\frac{1}{8}$ in. plywood can be used for the roof. The animals are cut from $\frac{1}{4}$ in. or $\frac{3}{8}$ in. plywood.

METHOD

The ark (Fig. 1) is made in three parts: (a) the hull, (b) the superstructure and (c) the roof (Fig. 2). All three parts are separate so that the ark can be assembled or taken apart at will.

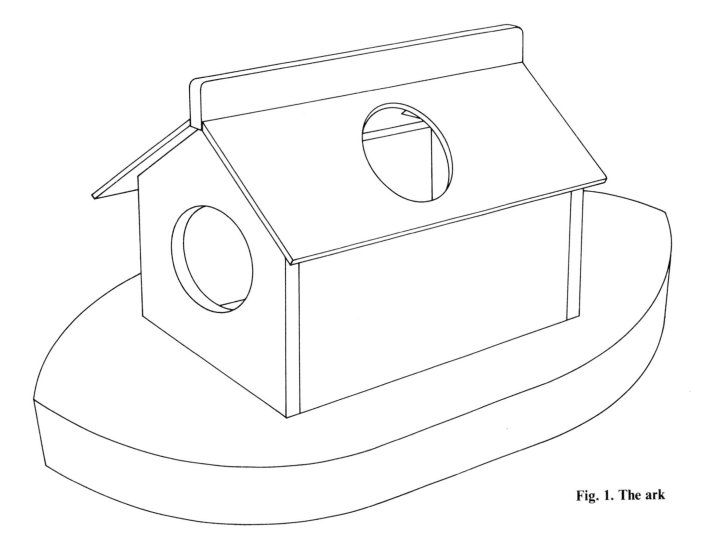

Fig. 1. The ark

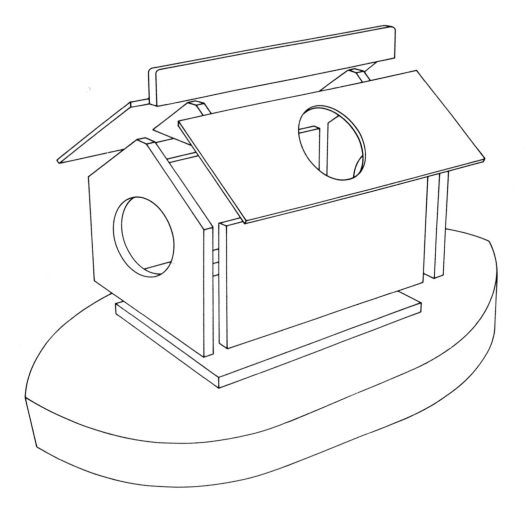

Fig. 2. The ark: components

The hull

The hull is made from three or, if you prefer, four thicknesses of plywood glued together. Cut each to the correct shape and size as shown in Fig. 3. The grid represents 1 in. squares. Draw your own grid of 1 in. squares and transfer the shape by marking with dots on your grid each point where the lines of the hull shape illustrated crosses the lines of the grid of Fig. 3. Join up the dots, taking care to follow the curves of the shape shown. Transfer to the wood. It will be found easier to cut the layers into shape before gluing. Spread the adhesive thinly on both surfaces to be joined and allow it to become tacky before placing them together. A couple of 'G' clamps with some waste plywood or hardboard to protect the hull will help to hold the sections together while the adhesive is drying; or anything heavy, such as a pile of old books, can be used.

The sides of the hull can now be sanded smooth and rounded off on the bottom edge, as shown in Figs. 4 and 5. Sand the top surface of the hull smooth before gluing the plywood locating panel in the position shown in Fig. 3. It is most important that the locating panel should be slightly smaller than the inner dimensions of the superstructure in order to allow easy assembly of the ark by small hands.

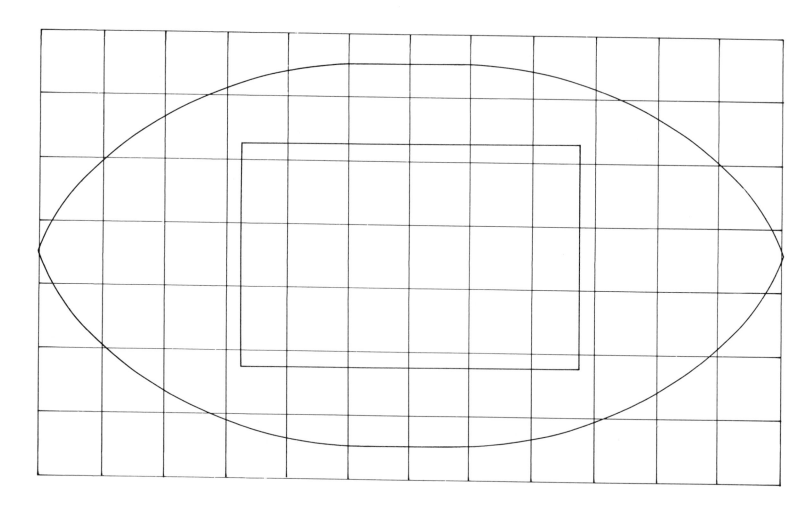

Fig. 3. Hull, plan view. Grid shows 1 in. squares

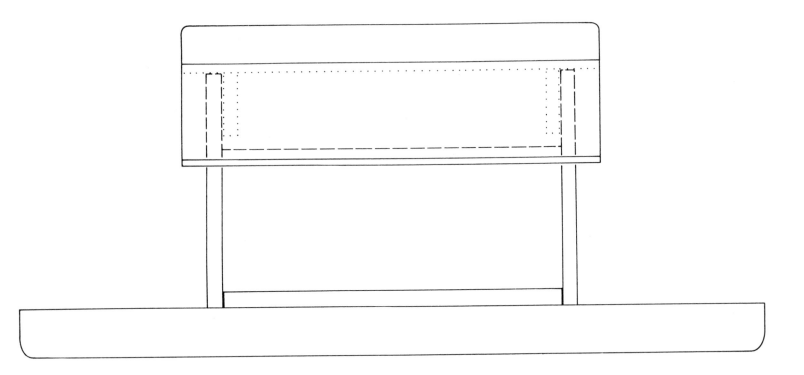

Fig. 4. Ark, side view.

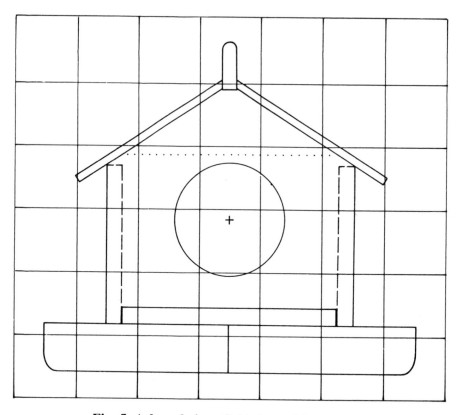

Fig. 5. Ark, end view. Grid shows 1 in. squares

The superstructure

Cut out the four pieces for the walls. Use Fig. 4 to obtain the sizes for the longer walls and Fig. 5 those for the two shorter end walls. The grids will show the correct dimensions. Take great care that all edges are straight and square and that all right-angled corners are accurate.

To cut the circular windows in the end panels, first drill a hole within the circle marked on Fig. 5. It should be large enough to accommodate the blade of your fretsaw or coping saw easily. Cut out the window as for the truck windows described on p. 39. This operation can be made easier if the sawing block described on p. 9 is used. Hints on using a fretsaw are given on p. 8.

The edges of the windows can be sanded smooth with sandpaper wrapped round a piece of dowel or cardboard tubing. Sand smooth all four pieces, taking great care to keep all edges and corners square. Then glue and pin the four pieces together as shown in Fig. 6. It is most important that the frame made by the four sides fits easily over the locating panel on the hull.

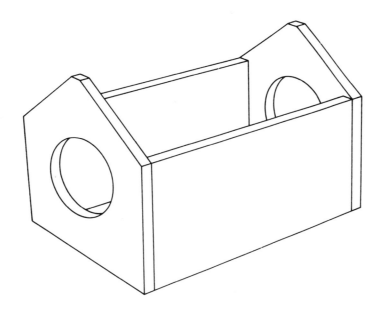

Fig. 6. Ark superstructure: walls assembled

The roof

Cut out the five pieces shown in Figs. 2, 4 and 5, using $\frac{1}{4}$ in. plywood for the ridge piece and the end pieces and $\frac{1}{8}$ in. hardboard or $\frac{1}{8}$ in. plywood for the roof slopes. The slopes are each $6\frac{3}{4}$ in. $\times$ $2\frac{3}{4}$ in. The other sizes can readily be taken from Figs. 4 and 5 by using the grids.

The roof window for the giraffes is cut out in exactly the same way as the end windows in the superstructure walls.

Assemble the roof as shown in Fig. 7. The triangular strengthening pieces at the ends also act as locating edges for the inner sides of the end pieces of the superstructure. As with the base of the superstructure and the locating panel on the hull, the roof must be a slightly loose fit on the superstructure so that small fingers can easily remove and replace the roof as a lid.

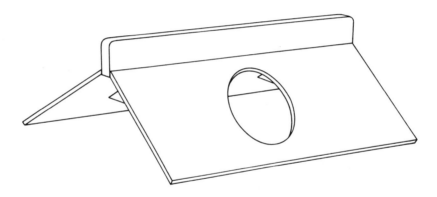

Fig. 7. Roof assembly

The animals and Mr and Mrs Noah

Trace the shapes shown in Figs. 8, 9, 10, 11 and 12 and transfer them to the plywood. The use of the sawing block mentioned above and described on p. 9 will facilitate the operation of cutting them out. Cut them out singly or in pairs from small pieces of plywood, and sand the edges smooth. If you wish to use ½ in. plywood for the figures, you must double the size of the ark.

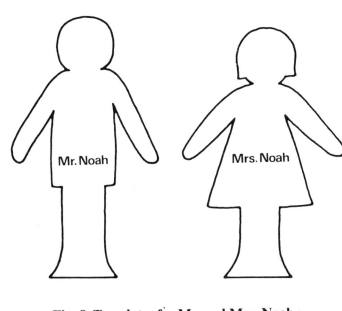

Fig. 8. Templates for Mr. and Mrs. Noah and animals. Full size

Fig. 9. Templates for animals. Full size

Dromedary

Cat

Lion

Rabbit

Cock

Fox

Polar Bear

Lamb

Fig. 10. Templates for animals. Full size

Giraffe

Pelican

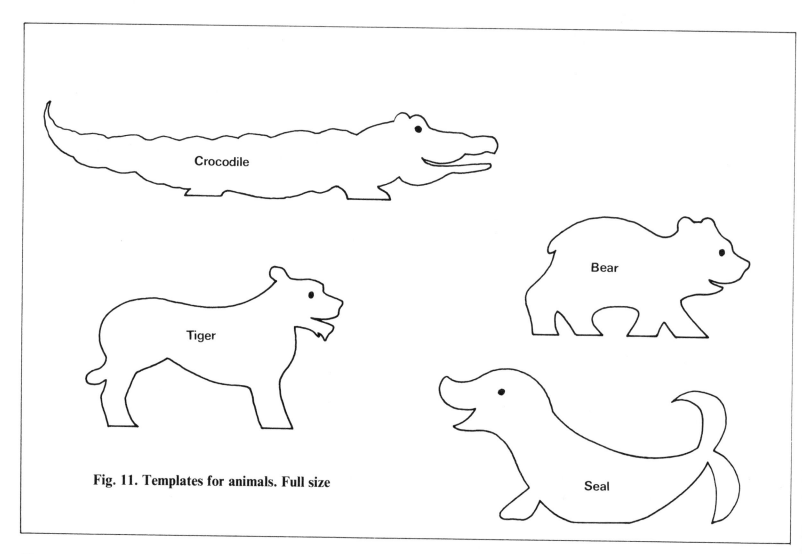

Fig. 11. Templates for animals. Full size

Cow

Elephant

Dog

Horse

Fig. 12. Templates for animals. Full size

Finishing and painting or varnishing

When sanding the ark and animals before painting or varnishing, you may find it useful to glue a piece of very fine sandpaper to a flat piece of board. Gently and smoothly rub the surface to be sanded against the prepared board, taking great care not to round off any edges or corners. It cannot be stressed enough that with the larger flat surfaces you must always work *with* the grain. Sanding across the grain causes scratches which take a long time to remove and which show up even more beneath varnish, polish, or dye. Care must also be taken not to split the end grains of the plywood by rubbing too hard or using too coarse a sandpaper.

The animals are best finished with three coats of clear varnish, the first coat being thinned sufficiently to seal the surface of the plywood. If you prefer bright colours, remember that the animals will continually be jolted and banged together; it would therefore be better to treat them with wood dyes or to stain them than to use ordinary paint. The eyes can be spotted on with a matchstick and black ink before dyeing or varnishing. Alternatively, use black enamel or paint if you are painting the animals, and apply after the main shade has dried. Mr. and Mrs. Noah may also be varnished or gaily painted.

Remember to use non-toxic paints or dyes.

Pull-along snake
and alligator

TOOLS

Tenon saw
Fretsaw or coping saw
Brace and bit or drill
$\frac{1}{2}$ in. chisel and mallet
Sandpaper (strips can be glued to small pieces of wood or card
    to make files)
Paintbrushes (including a small brush from a children's
    paintbox)

MATERIALS

Both the snake and the alligator jointed body sections are made
from $\frac{5}{8}$ in. plywood. Any thickness above $\frac{5}{8}$ in. may be used but
any thinner plywood would make the hinged joints too weak.
The wheels are 1 in. slices of $1\frac{1}{4}$ in. dowel, but wooden cotton
reels (if they can be found) or wheels cut from plywood (several
thicknesses glued together to make a minimum thickness of
1 in.) will do just as well. The axles and hinge pins are simply
short lengths of $\frac{1}{4}$ in. diameter wooden dowel. The cords for
pulling the toy along are of nylon upholstery cord, with a large
wooden curtain ring or a $2\frac{1}{2}$ in. length of $\frac{3}{8}$ in. diameter dowel as
a handle. You will also need a small chrome screw-in eye hook.

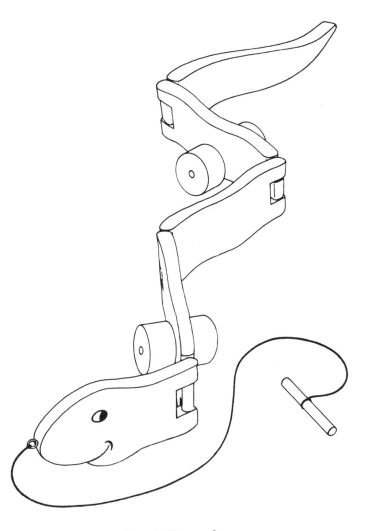

Fig. 1. The snake

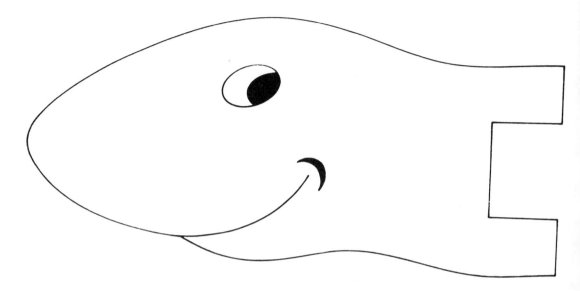

Fig. 2. Snake: head section. Full size

METHOD

Snake

Trace the head (Fig. 2), body (Fig. 3) and tail (Fig. 4) from the illustrations and transfer the outlines to the plywood. The middle (body) sections are all identical. You will need at least three of them. Should you wish to make the snake even longer, then sections must be added in pairs, each alternate section having an axle and wheels. To facilitate cutting out the pieces, a sawing block can easily be made out of an odd piece of plywood

as described on p. 9. Hints on using a fretsaw are given on p. 8.

Sand smooth all the sections, making sure that they all fit together tightly with no raised end edges spoiling the smoothness of the body curves. Do not at this point round off the hinges. Number all the parts so that none of the middle sections change places, which might spoil the fit or the shape of the snake when it is assembled.

The holes for the dowel hinge pins must now be drilled, making sure that the drill enters the upper hinge and passes

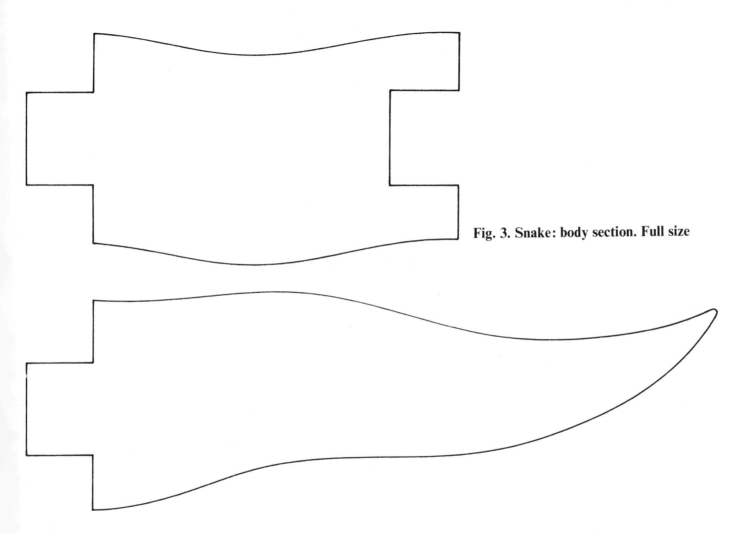

Fig. 3. Snake: body section. Full size

Fig. 4. Snake: tail section. Full size

centrally through the centre and bottom hinges (Fig. 5). Check that the dowel hinge pin fits firmly through all three holes in a perfectly straight and perpendicular line (Fig. 6a). The end edges of the hinges may now be rounded off to enable the two body sections to swivel (Fig. 6b). Check that the two pieces move without catching by inserting the hinge pin. *Do not at this stage loosen the hinge pin in any of the holes*. Repeat the complete operation for each of the hinges.

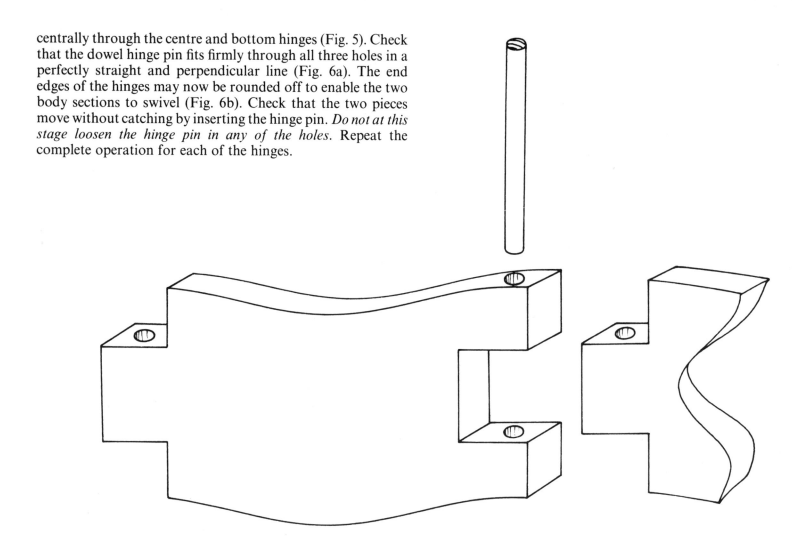

Fig. 5. Hinge dowel

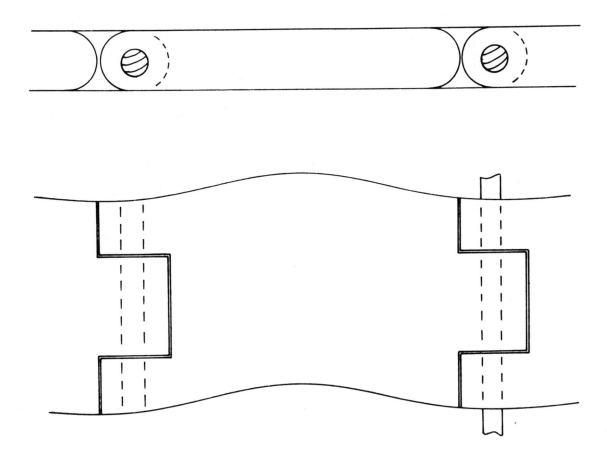

Fig. 6. Hinge assembled

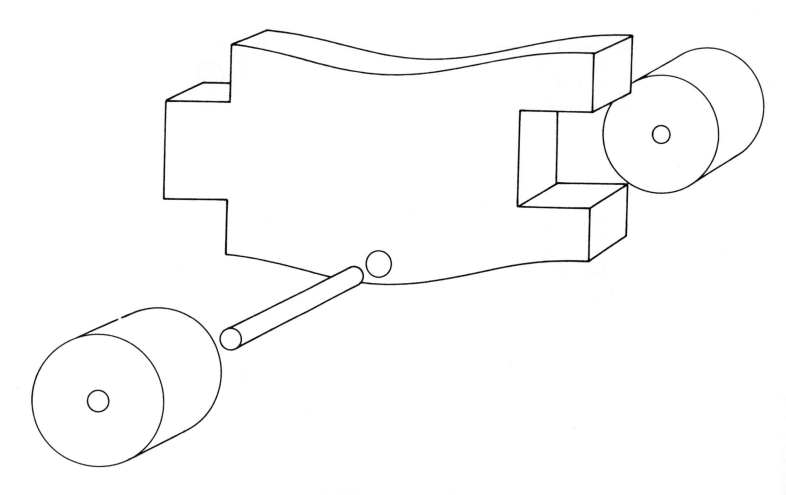

Fig. 7. Wheels and axles

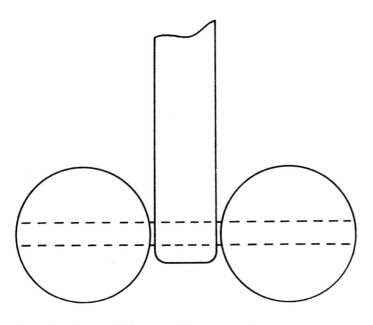

Fig. 8. Balls used as wheels

The holes for the axles may now be drilled in every other middle section, making sure that the axle dowel moves freely within them (Fig. 7).

The wheels are 1 in. thick slices of $1\frac{1}{4}$ in. dowel with a hole drilled centrally for the axle. *The axles must be a tight fit in the wheels*. Wooden balls of $1\frac{1}{4}$ to $1\frac{1}{2}$ in. diameter also make admirable wheels, but care must be taken to ensure that the holes for the axles are drilled centrally through them (Fig. 8). Should you wish the snake to bob up and down as it is pulled

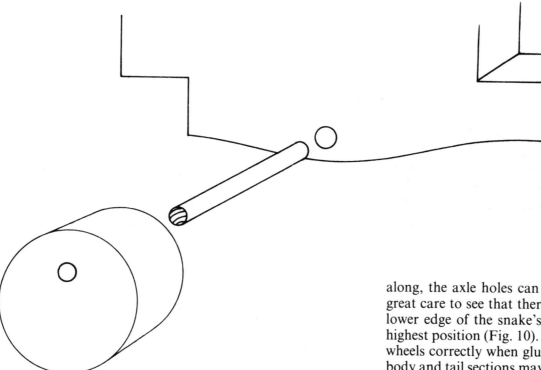

Fig. 9. Eccentric wheels

along, the axle holes can be drilled off centre (Fig. 9). Take great care to see that there is sufficient clearance between the lower edge of the snake's body when the wheels are in their highest position (Fig. 10). Care must also be taken to align the wheels correctly when gluing them on to the axles. The head, body and tail sections may now be assembled. You may find it easier to paint the sections before assembly.

The hinge pins are glued into the top and bottom sections of each hinge with the centre part of the hinge swivelling easily on the fixed hinge pin. The hole in the centre section of the hinge must therefore be enlarged slightly. This is easily done with a piece of tightly rolled sandpaper or even by using a slightly oversize drill. The protruding ends of the hinge pins are then removed and the surfaces sanded smooth (Fig. 5b).

68

Sand smooth and round off slightly the upper and lower edges of the assembled snake and paint it to your choice – if you have not already done so earlier. Do not allow any paint to run between the upper and lower surfaces of the hinge sections that slide against each other. The details of the face can be painted on with the small brush (see Fig. 2). When the paint has dried, the axles and wheels may be put into position. *Do not glue the wheels on to the axles at this stage.* Remove the axles and wheels from the snake and paint the wheels.

When dry, the axles may be glued into position on one wheel only. Insert the axles through the axle holes and glue the wheels on the other side. The axle ends may be left unpainted in the centre of each wheel, or a dab of contrasting or matching paint applied.

All that is now needed to finish the snake is the cord and handle with which to pull it along. A small chrome eye hook is screwed into the 'nose' of the snake with a 1½ ft. to 2 ft. length of coloured cord knotted into it. The other end of the cord can be knotted into a large curtain ring of a piece of ⅜ in. diameter dowel about 2½ in. long (see Fig. 1). The handle can of course be painted or varnished.

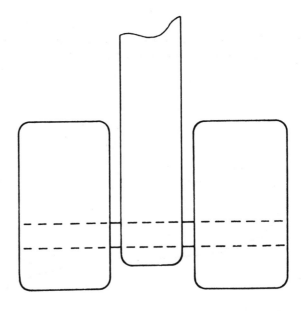

Fig. 10. Ground clearance with eccentric wheel

Alligator

Trace the body section plans from Figs. 12, 13 and 14, and transfer the outlines to the plywood. Using the sawing block (Fig. 15) cut out the sections as for the snake. Should you wish to make the aligator longer, two extra middle sections will be needed with an axle and wheels on the centre of the three middle sections. The details of the hinges and assembly are exactly as for the snake. Paint and finish the alligator to your choice.

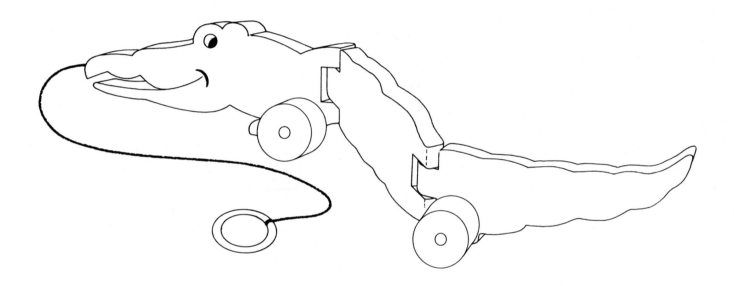

Fig. 11. The alligator

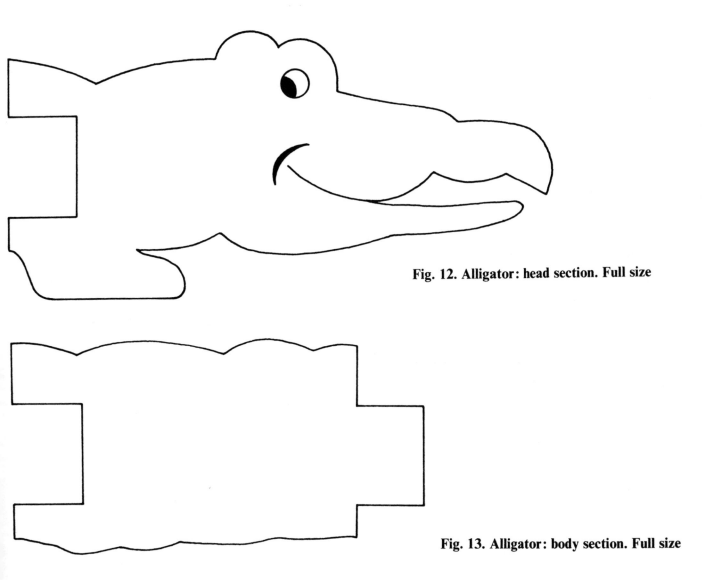

Fig. 12. Alligator: head section. Full size

Fig. 13. Alligator: body section. Full size

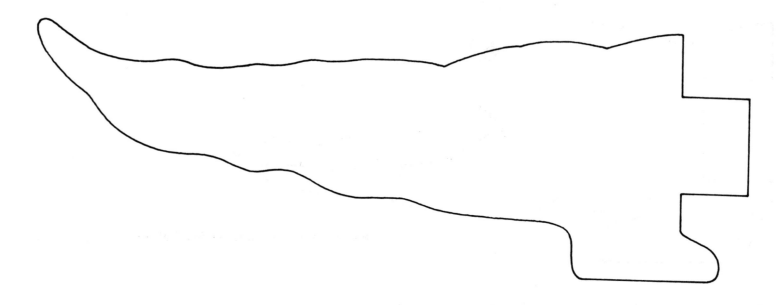

Fig. 14. Alligator: tail section. Full size

Farmyard

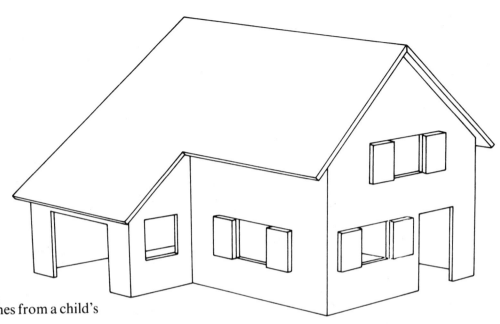

Fig. 1. The farmhouse

TOOLS

Try square
Tenon saw
Fretsaw or coping saw
Chisel and mallet
Craft knife
Hammer
Sandpaper
Paintbrushes (including a couple of paintbrushes from a child's
  paintbox)

MATERIALS

The farmhouse (Figs. 1 and 2) and the baseboard can be of
hardboard or thin plywood. The farmhouse templates (Figs. 3
and 4) are drawn for construction in hardboard. Should you

73

Fig. 2. Farmhouse: components

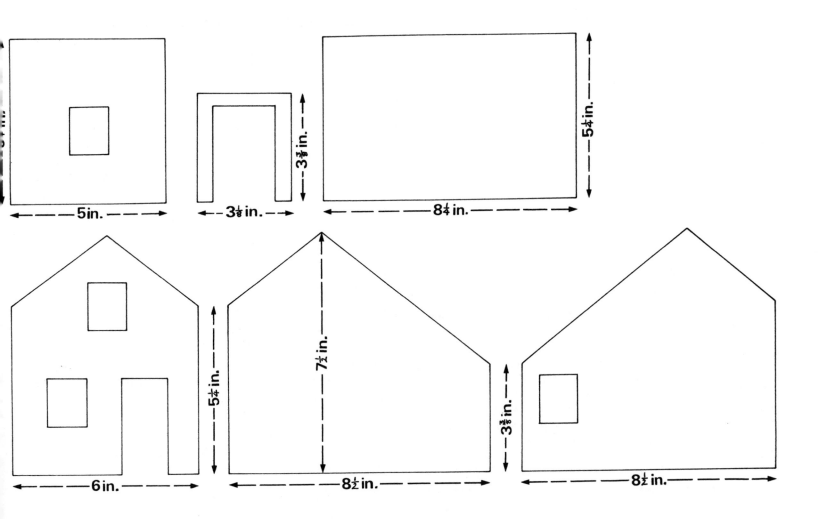

Fig. 3. Templates for walls

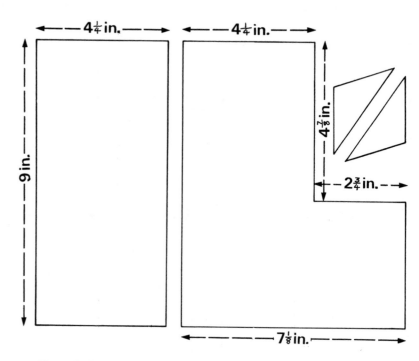

Fig. 4. Templates for roof

use plywood of greater thickness than $\frac{1}{8}$ in., allowance must be made by reducing the side walls and barn door accordingly.

The baseboard can be of any size required but should not be smaller than 24 in. × 18 in. At this size, hardboard is quite adequate, but for any much larger size plywood must be used to prevent the baseboard from 'bowing'. Even for quite a large baseboard, plywood thicker than $\frac{1}{4}$ in. is not necessary.

The farmer, his wife and the farm animals are cut from $\frac{3}{8}$ in. or $\frac{1}{2}$ in. plywood, although thinner plywood may be used with thin bases glued on in exactly the same way as the fence sections (Figs. 9 and 10).

The fences can be cut from thin wood or card (wood from a discarded cigar box is quite suitable) and can be made in any size or quantity to suit the size of the baseboard. By keeping the fence sections separate the farmer's fields may be altered in size and shape at will.

METHOD

The farmhouse

The wall sections are glued and pinned into position with lengths of $\frac{1}{2}$ in. square softwood batten. The roof sections are

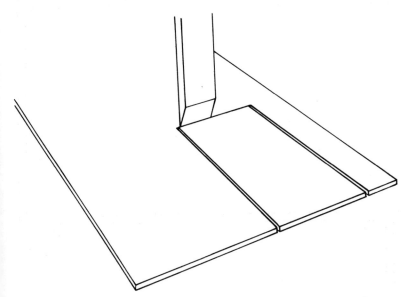

Fig. 5. Method of cutting doorway apertures

held in position by two triangular pieces of softwood, which when assembled correctly slot between the front and back walls to form a 'lid'. Cut all the pieces shown on the templates (Figs. 3 and 4), which are half full size. The two triangular pieces shown in Fig. 4 serve to strengthen the roof and must be cut from softwood at least $\frac{1}{2}$ in. thick.

The windows can be cut out with a chisel and mallet and then cleaned up with the craft knife and sandpaper. Take great care not to split the hardboard or plywood at the thinnest points. The doorway apertures are easily cut out by sawing the perpendicular edges and removing the waste along the upper edge with the chisel and mallet (Fig. 5).

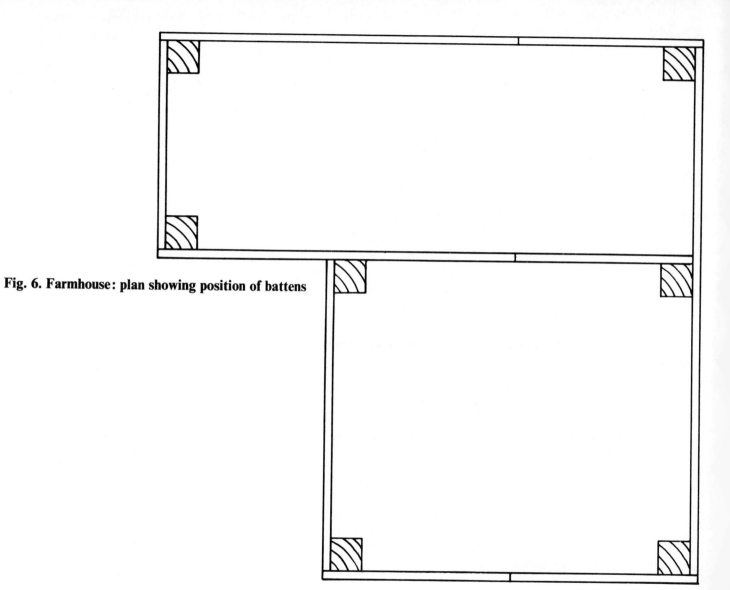

Fig. 6. Farmhouse: plan showing position of battens

The walls are glued and pinned together with five $5\frac{1}{4}$ in. lengths and two $2\frac{1}{4}$ in. lengths of $\frac{1}{2}$ in. square batten. The positions of the walls and battens are shown in the farmhouse plan (Fig. 6). Care must be taken that the walls are slotted into their correct positions, for incorrect assembly will result in a structure which is not square and upon which the roof will not sit squarely.

The window shutters are simply $1\frac{1}{4}$ in. $\times \frac{3}{4}$ in. rectangles of hardboard or $\frac{1}{8}$ in. plywood. These are glued into position on each side of the window apertures (Fig. 7). It will be found easier and tidier to paint the shutters first and to glue them into position after the walls have been painted.

The roof sections are sanded at an angle along both the apex edges so that they fit tightly together when glued and pinned into position with the triangular blocks (Fig. 8). Take care to ensure that the blocks fit firmly between the two outer walls

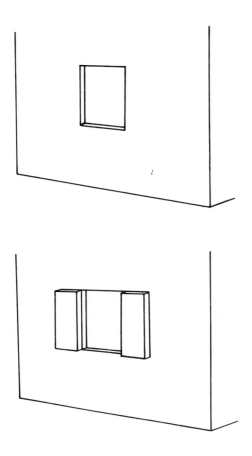

Fig. 7. Window shutters

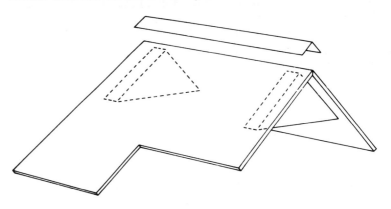

Fig. 8. Roof

and that the roof structure is positioned centrally with an equal overhang at each end. A strip of fabric 1 in. wide can be glued along the roof apex to make the structure even stronger (Fig. 8).

The farmhouse is now ready for painting. White emulsion paint will do beautifully for the walls with a contrasting gloss paint for the window shutters. If a painted 'pebble-dash' effect is wanted, non-drip emulsion paint can be stippled or daubed on to give a suitable finish. The roof can be painted in a gloss paint with a stippled and daubed undercoat if a thatched roof effect is required.

The baseboard

The baseboard is simply a rectangle of hardboard or plywood of a minimum size of 24 in. × 18 in. with a 'pond' and 'grass' painted in a gloss or matt finish. Paths can be painted if required, but a completely green area allows the farmhouse to be placed in a variety of positions during play. The pond can be cut from a piece of blue vinyl or similar material and also moved about the base area if desired. The baseboard can in fact be painted and finished exactly as you wish.

The fences

The fence sections (Fig. 9) are made separately to enable them to be placed in a variety of positions to form fields or enclosures of varying shapes and sizes. The upright posts are 2 in. lengths of $\frac{1}{8}$ in. $\frac{3}{16}$ in. × $\frac{1}{4}$ in. wood (cedarwood is ideal and varnishes beautifully) rounded at the top. The crossbars are 7 in. lengths of $\frac{1}{16}$ in. wood or card $\frac{3}{16}$ in wide. The centre bar should be slightly longer so that it can be trimmed off flush with the upright posts when glued into position. The base pieces are $\frac{3}{4}$ in. lengths of the same material as the crossbars. Glue the sections together as illustrated in Fig. 10 and paint or varnish to finish.

Should shorter lengths of fence be required, cut $3\frac{1}{2}$ in. lengths of crossbar and use only two posts for each fence section. (Remember to allow extra length for the inclined centre bar.)

The farmer, his wife and the animals

The templates for the figures and animals (Figs. 11–13) are full size and can be traced directly on to $\frac{3}{8}$–$\frac{1}{2}$ in. plywood. The shapes are simple and are quite easily cut out with a fretsaw or coping saw. A sawing block made from an odd piece of plywood as described in the Introduction (p. 9). For hints on using a fretsaw, see p. 8. Cut the figures or animals out singly or in pairs from small pieces of plywood. As the blades and teeth of a fretsaw and coping saw are fine there will be no difficulty in sanding the edges smooth. 'Files' can be made by gluing small pieces of sandpaper to pieces of hardboard and dowel or even wrapping them round a pencil.

The figures and animals can be painted or varnished. Should you wish to paint them in bright colours remember that they will continually be jolted and banged together and would therefore be better if treated with wood dyes or stain. The eyes and detail can easily be applied with the small brushes. *Take great care to use non-toxic paints or dyes.*

The farmyard is now ready. It can easily be added to when desired.

Simple trees and bushes can be cut from plywood of the same thickness as the animals. A large barn can be made by adapting the farmhouse templates, and smaller fences for a chicken run, etc. 'Stone' walls can be made from lengths of $1\frac{1}{2}$–2 in. × $\frac{1}{8}$ in.–$\frac{1}{2}$ in. timber, painted and finished in the same way as the farmhouse walls. The instructions in this book are intended only for a basic farmyard, but there is no end to the improvements and adaptations that are possible with this toy.

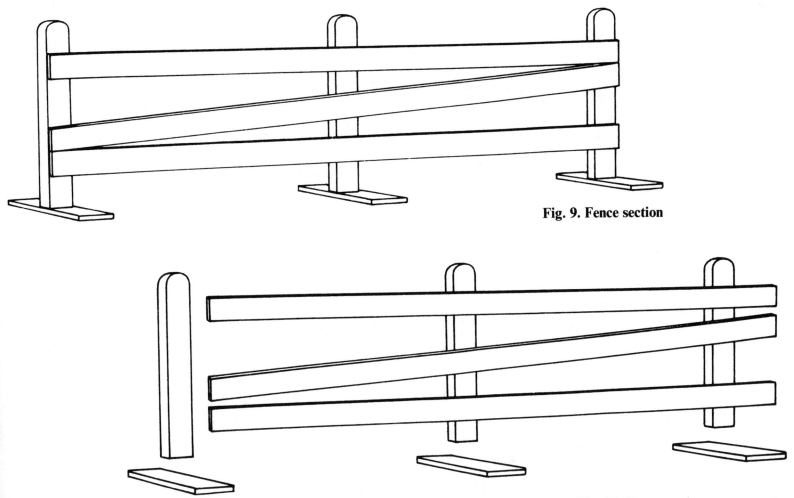

Fig. 9. Fence section

Fig. 10. Fence section: components

81

Fig. 11. Templates for farmer, farmer's wife and animals

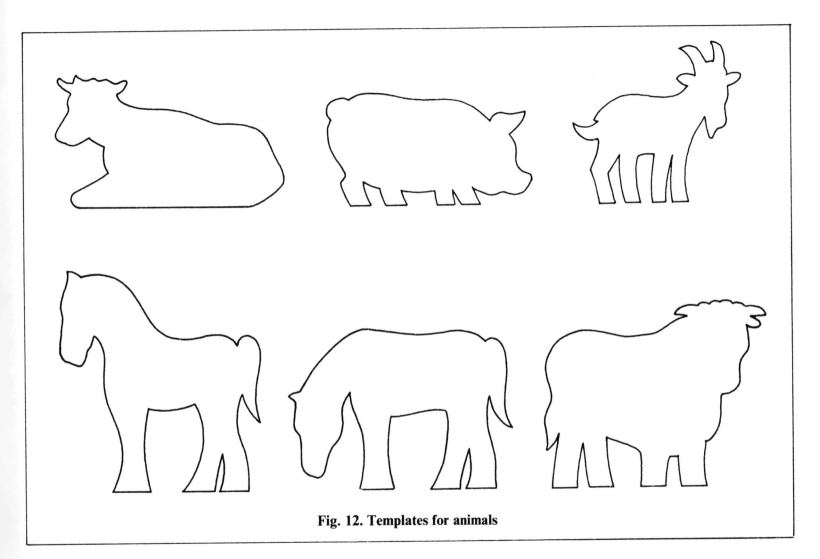

Fig. 12. Templates for animals

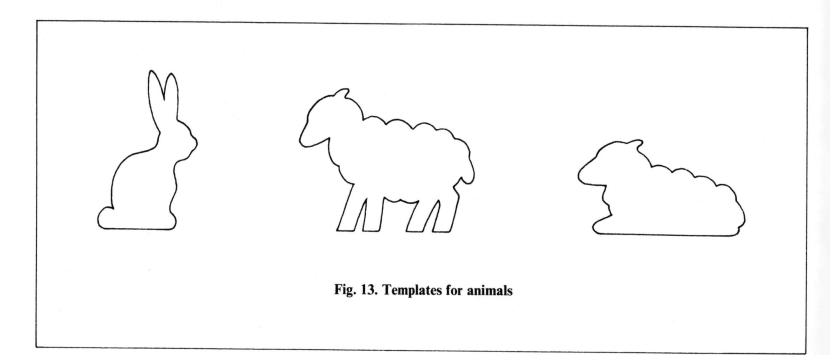

Fig. 13. Templates for animals

Play tunnel

TOOLS

Tenon saw
Keyhole or pad saw
Brace and bit (or hand drill)
Sandpaper
Paintbrushes

MATERIALS

The play tunnel (Fig. 1) is made entirely from $\frac{1}{8}$ in. hardboard panels of square and rectangular shape laced together with upholstery cord through holes drilled at the edges of each of the panels. Circular apertures are cut in some of the panels to facilitate entry and exit in a wide variety of positions for an even wider variety of make-believe games.

METHOD

The play tunnel panels are cut from $\frac{1}{8}$ in. hardboard, the smaller panels being 20 in. × 20 in. and the larger ones 20 in. × 40 in. Ten panels are required (Fig. 2) to make up the basic L-shaped tunnel (Fig. 3). Holes $\frac{3}{16}$ in. in diameter are drilled at regular intervals $\frac{3}{4}$ in. from the outer edges of the panels. Five holes in each side of a square panel and in the ends of a rectangular panel are quite sufficient; they are spaced $4\frac{5}{8}$ in. apart at their

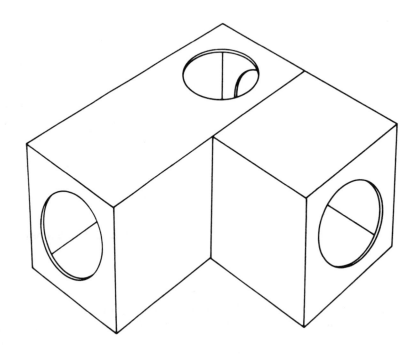

Fig. 1. The basic play tunnel

85

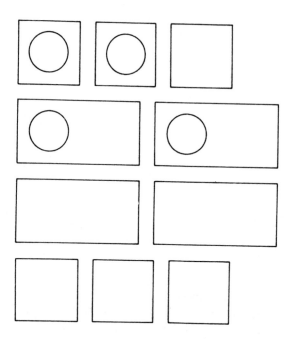

Fig. 2. The ten panels for the basic tunnel

centres. The holes in the long sides of the rectangular panels are nine in number and are approximately $4\frac{3}{4}$ in. apart at their centres.

The circular apertures are first marked by finding the centres of the panels and scribing a circle of 15 in. diameter ($7\frac{1}{2}$ in. radius) in each. To find the centre of a 20 in. × 20 in. panel, draw a straight line from one corner to the opposite corner and repeat for the other two corners. Where the lines cross is the central point from which to scribe the circle. In the case of the larger panels first measure half the length of the longer sides and draw a line across the panel to give an exact square in which to repeat the 'centre-finding' procedure. A simple device for scribing the circles can be made from an 8 in. or 9 in. length of hardboard approximately 1 in. wide. Drill a hole in the

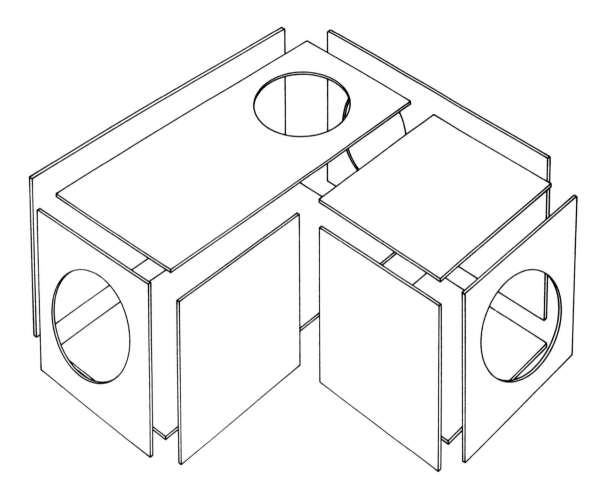

Fig. 3. Panels: assembly

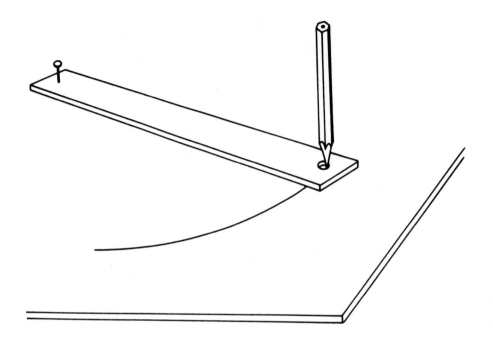

Fig. 4. Device for scribing circles

centre of one end of this, large enough to take a pencil point. At a point $7\frac{1}{2}$ in. from the outer edge of the hole drive a nail through the hardboard strip into the centrally marked point on a hardboard panel. Swing the strip round a few times until it moves freely round the nail. Insert a pencil point into the hole and the circle is easily drawn (Fig. 4).

The circular apertures are cut out by first drilling, within the area to be removed, a hole large enough to accommodate the blade of the keyhole saw or pad-saw blade. The aperture can now easily be sawn out (Fig. 5).

Repeat the whole operation for each of the circular apertures and sand all edges smooth. All the corners of the panels can now be rounded off to an approximate radius of $\frac{3}{4}$ in. to prevent damage to the corners and to eliminate the possibility of

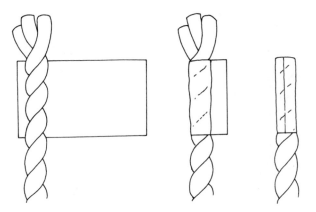

Fig. 6. Tags for cord

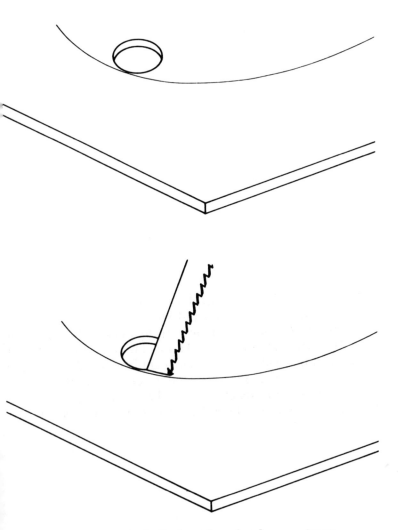

Fig. 5. Method of cutting circular apertures

toddlers hurting themselves on them during play.

The panels can now be painted in a variety of bright colours. When dry the panels are laced together with 36 in. and 72 in. lengths of upholstery cord or plastic-sheathed clothes line (*not* the metal wire type). The 36 in. lengths are used for lacing square panels and the ends of the rectangular panels. The 72 in. lengths of lacing are for the long sides of the rectangular panels.

If upholstery cord is used a 'tag' at each end will make the threading through the drilled holes easier. To make the tags, roll an inch or two of adhesive tape round the ends of the cord and trim the cord ends (Fig. 6).

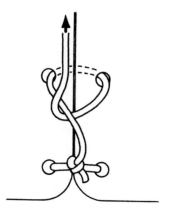

Fig. 7. Thonging stitch

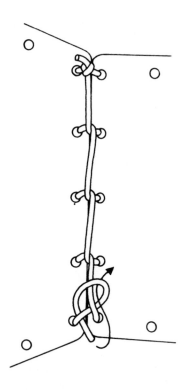

Fig. 8. Panels laced together

The lengths of cord are kept short to make the lacing and tying operation easier. Loop and knot the cord at one end of the panels to be joined and lace through in a thonging stitch (Fig. 7). Pull each loop tight and knot at the end (Fig. 8). Stand the play tunnel walls up and lace them from inside. The base can then be laced, and the top sections added one at a time so that the holes can be reached easily. The circular apertures will be found useful in reaching the corners of the very last panel.

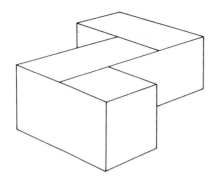

Fig. 9. Z-shaped tunnel

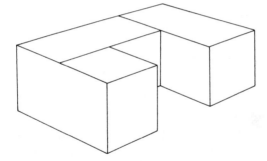

Fig. 10. U-shaped tunnel

To pack the play tunnel away when it is not in use it is unnecessary to dismantle all the panels completely. Remove the end panels of the tunnel and the 'L' section and the two structures can then be folded into a size that can easily be stacked away.

The addition of further panels will enable a wide variety of shapes to be made. Five additional panels will make an extra tunnel length to form a 'Z' shape (Fig. 9) or a 'U' shape (Fig. 10). With even more panels a continuous tunnel can be made (Fig. 11). The more rectangular panels there are the stronger and more easily assembled the tunnel becomes. Circular 'doors' and 'windows' can be positioned wherever required.

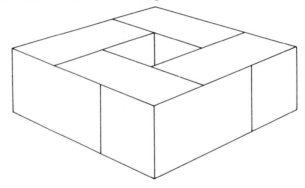

Fig. 11. Continuous tunnel

Wendy house

TOOLS

Tenon saw
Keyhole or narrow-bladed saw
Brace and bit or hand drill
Hammer (if nails are used) or screwdriver (if screws are used)
Sandpaper
Paintbrushes

MATERIALS

The Wendy house (Fig. 1) is made entirely from $\frac{1}{8}$ in. hardboard, with the exception of the window ledges, chimney-stack strengthening battens, and the chimney pots. The window ledges and chimney-stack battens are of $\frac{3}{4}$ in. × 1 in. softwood and the chimney pots are $2\frac{1}{2}$ in. lengths of $2\frac{1}{4}$ in. diameter cardboard tubing. (The diameter of the tubing is not, however, critical: any diameter will do as long as the chimney pots do not look too small or too large for the main structure.)

The walls are held together by lacing upholstery cord through holes drilled in the corner edges of each of the hardboard panels. The roof slopes are held together in exactly the same way and the same method is used to form a hinge for the door.

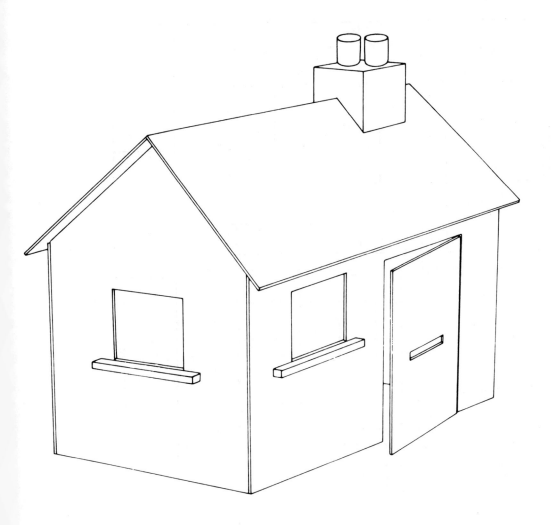

Fig. 1. The Wendy house

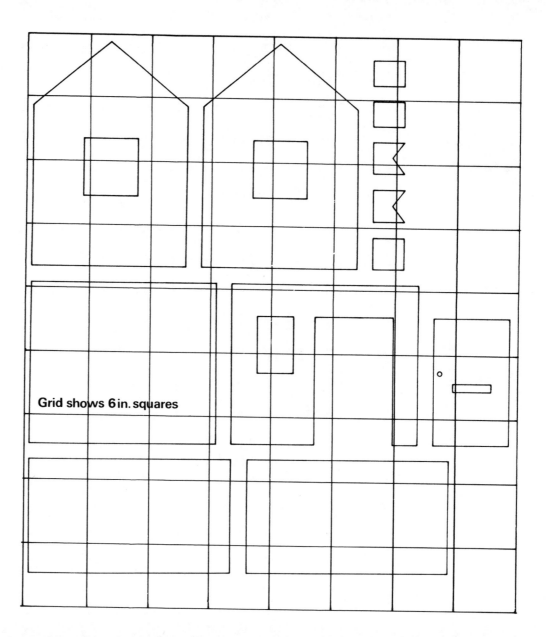

Fig. 2. Hardboard panels for Wendy house

Grid shows 6 in. squares

METHOD

The main structure

The panels to be cut from hardboard are shown in Fig. 2. The roof panels are 21 in. × 40 in. rectangles of ⅛ in. hardboard. The front and back walls are 30 in. × 36 in. The side walls are made from 40 in. × 30 in. rectangles. To form the apex of the side wall, mark points on either side of the long edges, 30 in. from the bottom, and another point exactly in the middle of the top short edge. Cut away the triangular pieces so formed.

The windows are cut out by first drilling, within the area to be removed, a hole large enough to accommodate the blade of the keyhole saw (Fig. 3). The window area can now easily be removed. Repeat the operation for each of the windows. The top edge of the door aperture can be cut in the same way, the upright edges being sawn with the tenon saw.

Carefully sand all edges and corners smooth, keeping edges straight and corners square.

The letter slot and finger hole in the door are cut in exactly the same way as the windows. Should you prefer a handle to the finger hole, remember that fixing must be from the back of the

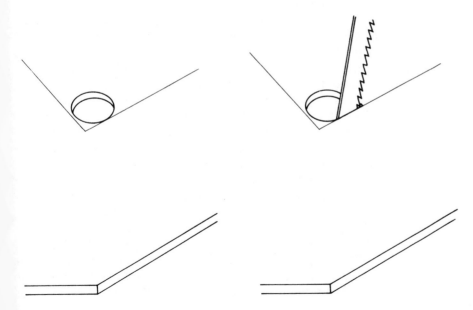

Fig. 3. Method of cutting out windows

hardboard into the handle. Never try to screw or nail into hardboard, only through it into whatever is being fixed.

The window ledges are lengths of $\frac{3}{4}$ in. × 1 in. batten, 3 in. wider than the window aperture. Fix each centrally beneath the window area, level with the bottom edge (Fig. 4).

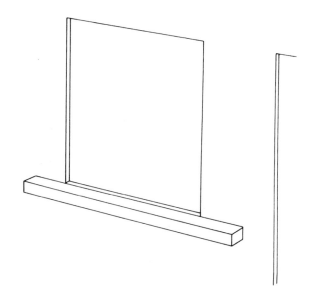

Fig. 4. Window ledges

The chimney-stack

The sides and top of the chimney-stack are cut from $\frac{1}{8}$ in. hardboard (Fig. 2). The top is 6 in. square; rectangular pieces 6 in. × $4\frac{3}{4}$ in. form two of the sides; the other two are pieces of 6 in. square cut as shown to fit the apex of the roof. The battens for reinforcing the corners are four 6 in. lengths of $\frac{3}{4}$ in. × 1 in. softwood each with one end cut at an angle to fit the roof. The stack is assembled and screwed or nailed as shown in Figs. 5 and 6. The chimneys are pieces of cardboard tubing $2\frac{1}{2}$ in. long glued to the top of the stack (Fig. 7).

Assembling the house

The next step is to drill the lacing holes in the wall ends. The holes should be $\frac{1}{4}$ in. in diameter, the top and bottom holes being 1 in. from their respective ends with the remaining holes at 4 in. intervals. The two roof slopes must be divided in exactly the same way along the apex sides, as should one side of the door and the hinge side of the door aperture. *Make sure that the holes in any panel line up with the holes in the next panel.*

The wall panels, roof, door and chimney are now ready to paint prior to assembly. The walls can be finished in washable emulsion paint, and the roof, chimney-stack, door and window ledges in gloss paint. A suitable finish is as follows: walls: white non-drip emulsion paint, daubed on and stippled to give a textured appearance; roof and chimney-stack: bright red gloss paint; door and window ledges: bright turquoise gloss paint; chimney pots: black gloss paint.

The house is assembled by lacing the panels together with lengths of upholstery cord. You will need a 51 in. length for each of the wall corners, 68 in. for the roof and 40 in. for the door. A stout cord should be used. Make a tag at each end as

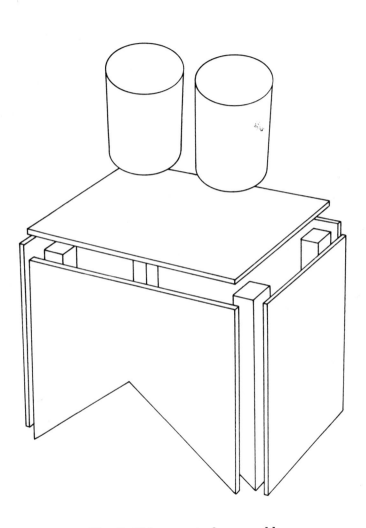

Fig. 5. Chimney-stack: assembly

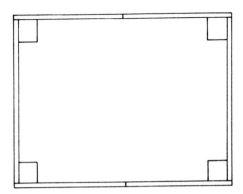

Fig. 6. Chimney-stack: corner battens

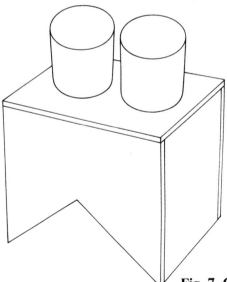

Fig. 7. Chimney-stack complete

97

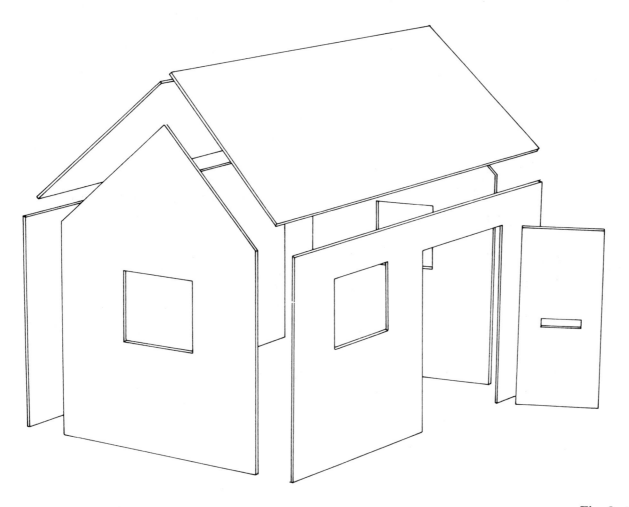

Fig. 8. Assembling the Wendy house

shown on p. 89 so that the cord can easily be threaded through the drilled holes.

The cord is looped and knotted at the bottom end and laced through in a thonging stitch, as shown on p. 90. Pull each loop tight and knot the cord at the top. Fig. 8 shows how the pieces fit together. It will be found easier to assemble the house if, after having laced the first corner, the walls are stood up and the other corners laced from inside. The door should be laced to the front wall before assembling it with the adjacent walls.

Lace together the roof slopes, place them in position centrally so that the ends protrude equally at each side, and put the chimney-stack on the apex of the roof.

The Wendy house is now ready. To pack it away when not in use, it is not necessary to dismantle all the panels completely. The roof slopes need only be folded and the back wall removed to enable the whole structure to be folded to a size that can easily be stacked away in a box-room or garden shed (Fig. 9).

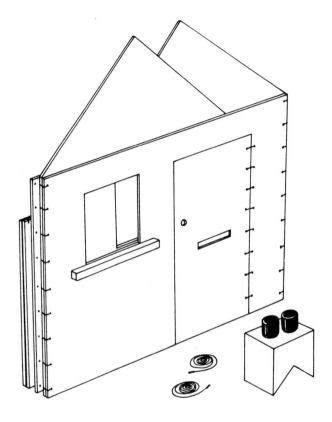

Fig. 9. Wendy house folded up for storage

Rocking horse and hobby horse

TOOLS

Tenon saw
Block plane or smoothing plane
Keyhole or narrow-bladed saw
Brace and bit or drill, and countersink bit
$\frac{1}{4}$ in. and/or $\frac{1}{2}$ in. chisels, and mallet
Screwdriver
Rasp
Sandpaper
Paintbrushes

Rocking horse

MATERIALS

With the exception of the body and handle, the entire rocking horse (Fig. 1) is cut from $\frac{1}{2}$ in. plywood. If greater strength is required, $\frac{3}{4}$ in. plywood can be used. The legs and rockers on each side are cut in one piece to eliminate difficult joints and to give the rocking horse more strength (Fig. 2). The head, tail and seat are relatively simple shapes, also cut from $\frac{1}{2}$ in. plywood. All five pieces are fixed to the body with $\frac{3}{4}$ in. to 1 in.

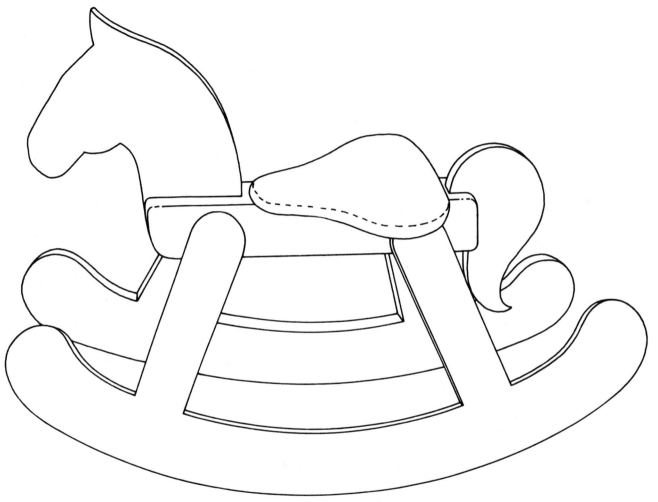

Fig. 1. The rocking horse

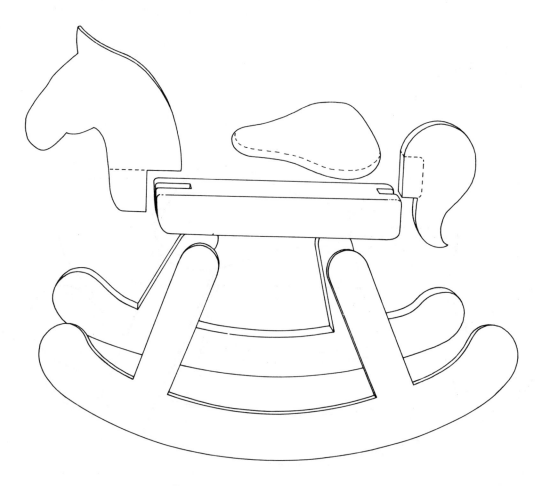

Fig. 2. Rocking horse: components

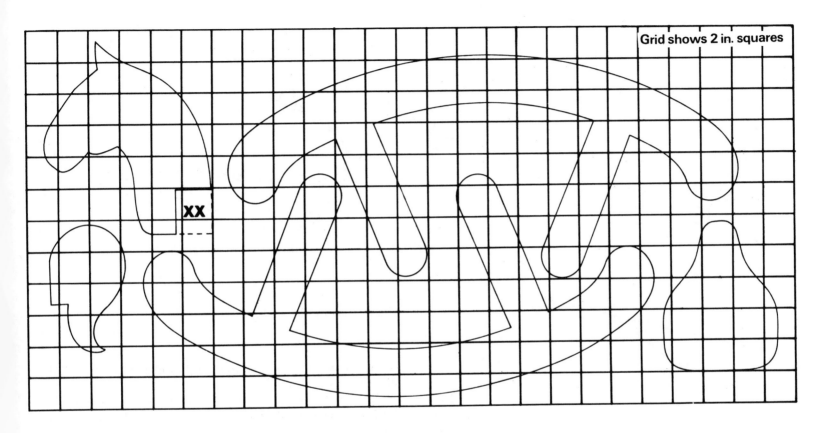

Fig. 3. Parts to be cut from $\frac{1}{2}$ in. plywood

XX

Grid shows 2 in. squares

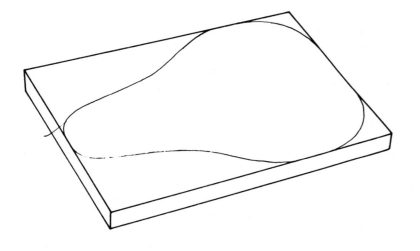

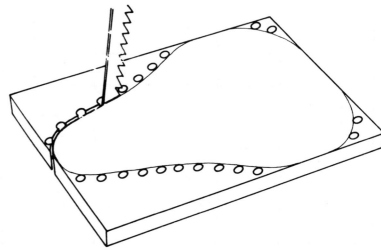

Fig. 4. Cutting the seat

screws, with the heads countersunk and filled with cellulose filler or plastic wood.

The body is a length of 3 in. × 2 in. timber, $16\frac{1}{2}$ in. long, with the 2 in. sides planed to an angle to splay the legs and rockers outwards.

You will also require an adhesive.

METHOD

Fig. 3 shows the parts to be cut from the $\frac{1}{2}$ in. plywood. Cut out the pieces with a keyhole or narrow-bladed saw. It may be

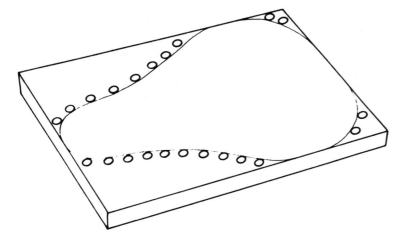

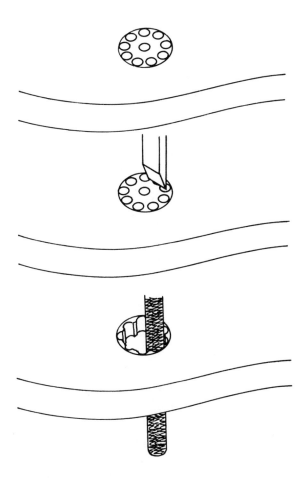

Fig. 5. Cutting hole for handle

found easier to drill a line of holes round the shapes before cutting. Cut from hole to hole as shown in Fig. 4. The ragged edge can then be removed with a rasp or with rough sandpaper before smoothing off for final assembly. Take great care to see that both sets of legs and rockers are identical. Cut away the section marked XX on Fig. 3.

The hole for the handle through the rocking horse's head can be drilled and smoothed as shown in Fig. 5. Make sure that you do not make the hole too large for the handle. This is a $7\frac{1}{2}$ in. length of 1 in. dowel or broom handle with both ends rounded and sanded smooth. The handle is then glued and screwed

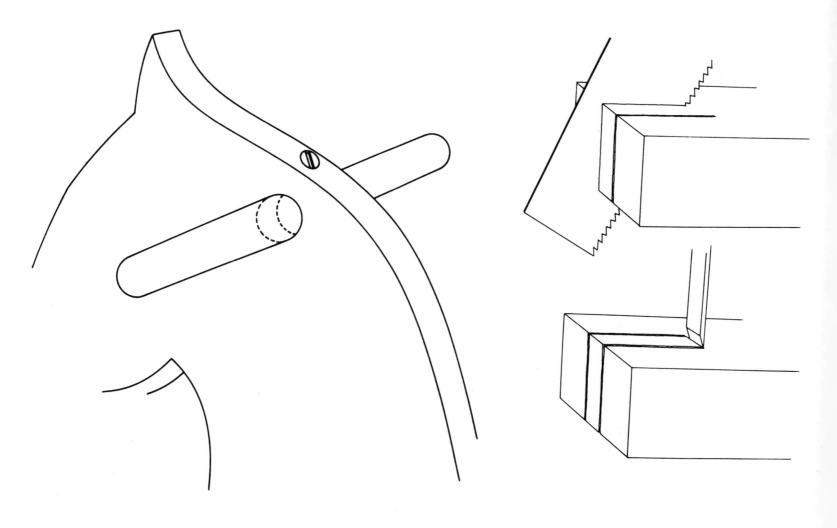

Fig. 6. Fitting handle in horse's head

Fig. 7. Cutting slots for head and tail

centrally into position as shown in Fig. 6. The screw head must be countersunk and the hole then filled with cellulose filler or plastic wood.

The rocking horse's body is a $16\frac{1}{2}$ in. length of 3 in. × 2 in. timber. The slots for the head and tail can be cut with a tenon saw and removed with a mallet and $\frac{1}{2}$ in. chisel (Fig. 7). The sides are planed or sawn so that the upper width is reduced by $\frac{1}{2}$ in. at each side, while the width of the underside remains 3 in. (Fig. 8).

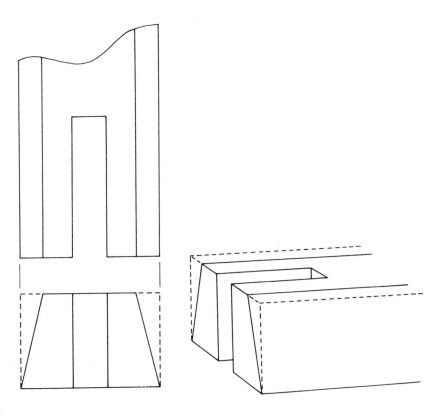

Fig. 8. Shaping the sides of the body

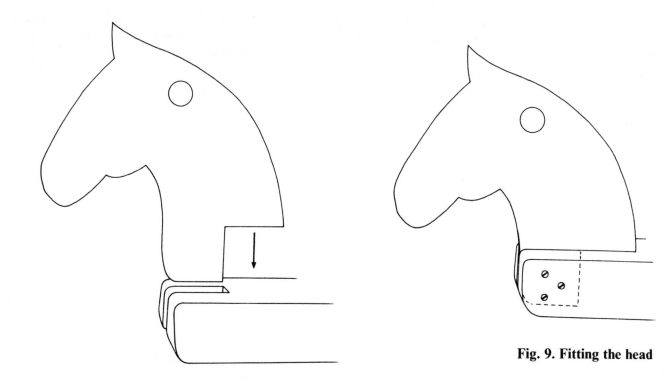

Fig. 9. Fitting the head

The head and tail can now be slotted and screwed into position (Figs. 9 and 10). Next, screw on the legs and rockers (Fig. 11). It cannot be stressed enough that all screw heads or ends must be countersunk and filled. *Any protruding screw heads or ends can be dangerous and must be smoothed off completely.*

108

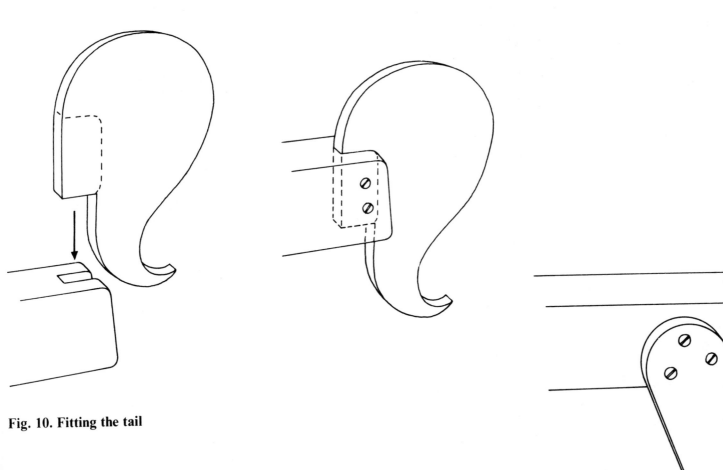

Fig. 10. Fitting the tail

Fig. 11. Fixing for leg

The seat can now be fitted and screwed into position centrally between the head and tail (Fig. 12). Check carefully that the rocking horse sits squarely and the rockers are lined up, making sure that one is not slightly in front of the other. Smooth off any rough edges, particularly on the seat and the head and tail. The rocking horse is now ready for painting. Suitable colours are a good white gloss for the head, body and legs, with the mane, eyes, nostrils, hooves and tail picked out in black. Fig. 14 gives some ideas for head detail. The rockers and handle can be painted bright red.

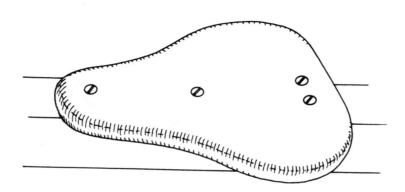

Fig. 12. Fixing for seat

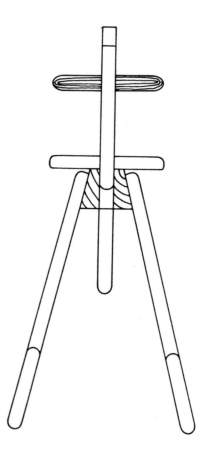

Fig. 13. End view with legs and seat fixed in position

Fig. 14. Details for painting head

Hobby horse

A simple hobby horse can be made, using the same head shape as for the rocking horse.

MATERIALS

As before, the head is of $\frac{1}{2}$ in. plywood. The body is made from two 30 in. lengths of $1\frac{1}{4}$ in. $\times$ $\frac{1}{4}$ in. batten, fixed at one end to both sides of the neck, and to the spacer block and wheel at the other as shown in Fig. 15. The spacer block is $1\frac{1}{4}$ in. $\times$ $1\frac{3}{4}$ in. $\times$ $\frac{1}{4}$ in. The wheel is $3\frac{1}{2}$ in. diameter and is cut from $\frac{5}{8}$ in. plywood. The axle is of $\frac{3}{8}$ in. dowel. For assembling the hobby horse $\frac{1}{2}$ in. screws are needed.

METHOD

Cut out the head as for the rocking horse, but do not cut away the section marked XX. This forms a locating tongue to fit into a slot in the body.

Drill a $\frac{3}{8}$ in. hole in the centre of the wheel and glue a $1\frac{1}{2}$ in. length of $\frac{3}{8}$ in. dowel in the hole so that $\frac{7}{16}$ in. protrudes at each side.

Carefully round off and smooth each end of both battens. Drill holes for the axle $1\frac{1}{4}$ in. from one end. They must be large enough to allow the $\frac{3}{8}$ in. axle to spin freely.

To assemble the hobby horse, fix *one* batten to the head and then fix the spacer block in the position shown in the illustration, using $\frac{1}{2}$ in. screws, countersunk and filled. Insert the axle on one side into the axle hole and place the other batten in position. Before screwing down this second batten, ensure that the wheel spins freely between the two battens, that they are in exactly corresponding positions on each side of the head, and that they are lined up evenly at the axle holes.

The handle is exactly the same as for the rocking horse. Fix it in position and paint the hobby horse to your choice. Once again Fig. 14 will help with the painting of the head.

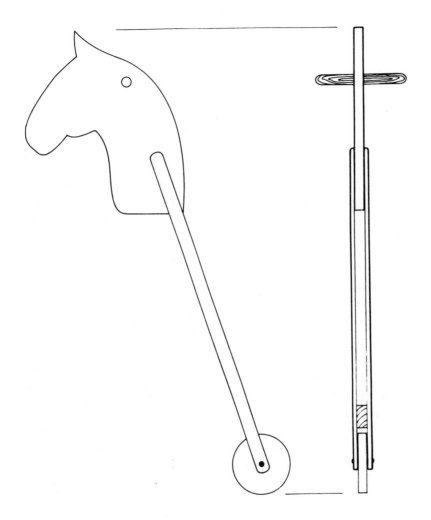

Fig. 15. Hobby horse

Go-cart

TOOLS

Saw
Try square
Hand or electric drill with $\frac{1}{16}$ in., $\frac{1}{4}$ in. and $\frac{7}{16}$ in. drills
Hacksaw
Flat file
Pliers
Hammer
Spanner (size according to that of nuts used on coach bolts)
Screwdriver
Sandpaper
Paintbrushes

MATERIALS

The go-cart is made from $\frac{3}{4}$ in. thick timber with 1 in. thick strengthening bars and is simply bolted together with $\frac{1}{4}$ in. diameter coach bolts of 2 in. to $2\frac{1}{2}$ in. lengths. The whole structure when correctly assembled is very strong but in the event of an accident a damaged part is easily replaced. The four wheels are all of the same size, 7 in. to 8 in. diameter, and should be as sturdy as possible. Most toy and hardware shops that stock wheels of this size also stock axles, but should there be any difficulty in obtaining them, instructions for making simple axles from mild steel tubing are given below. The steering rope is of polypropylene or nylon.

Special note

Read through *all* the instructions before drilling any assembly holes. You may find it easier to match holes drilled in the main structure with holes already drilled in the axles, or you may prefer to drill the holes in the main structure first. Check on the number of washers and nuts you require. Also check on the number of coach bolts needed, making sure that if you are using timber of different thicknesses to those specified, the bolts do not protrude too far or are too short to take locking washers and nuts. If you are using axles which are purchased with the wheels, or even wheels and axles from discarded toys, make sure that they are sturdy enough. If the axle has to be fixed with 'U' bolts or brackets, there must be axle stops to prevent side-to-side movement.

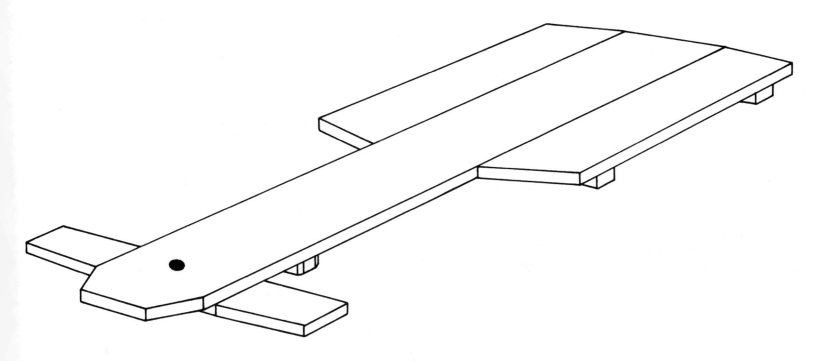

Fig. 1. The go-cart main frame or structure

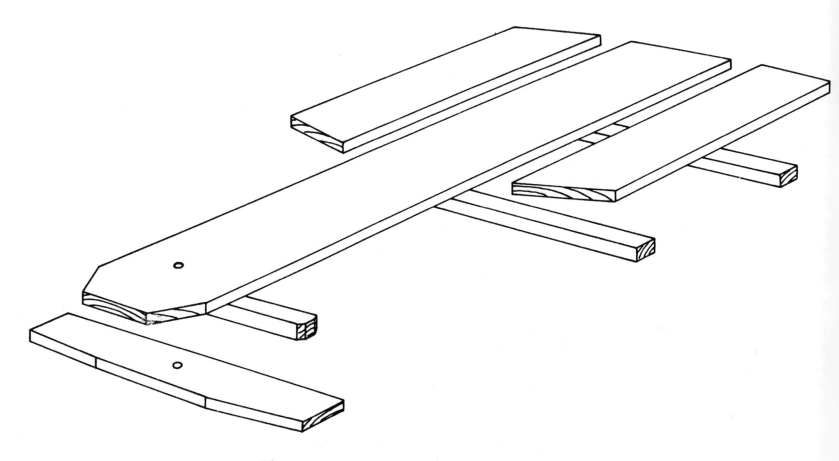

Fig. 2. Go-cart: components of main frame or structure

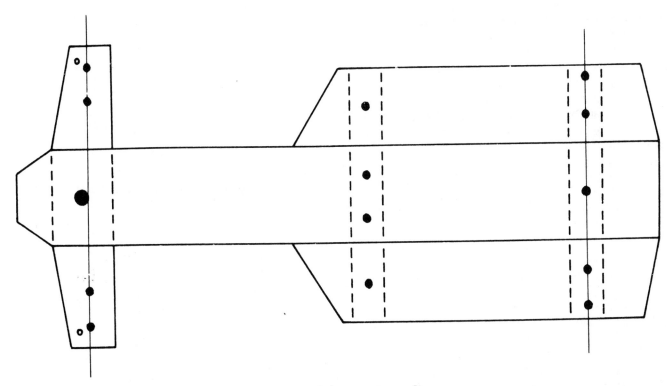

Fig. 3. Main structure: plan

METHOD

The main structure

The main structure is simply made from three shaped boards bolted together with the steering board pivoted to the front end (Figs. 1 and 2).

The centre board is a 42 in. length of $6\frac{1}{2}$ in. $\times$ $\frac{3}{4}$ in. timber with the two front end corners sawn off (see Fig. 3). To make the correct shape, measure a point $1\frac{3}{4}$ in. from a front corner along the side of the board. Mark another point $1\frac{3}{4}$ in. from the corner across the board and rule a line from one point to the other. Repeat for the other corner and remove the two pieces.

The two shaped side pieces are 24 in. lengths of $4\frac{3}{4}$ in. $\times$ $\frac{3}{4}$ in.

timber with the front and back ends sawn off at angles. The front end angle is arrived at by marking a point 3 in. from the front on the outer edge and ruling a line from the inner front corner to the marked point. The back end outer edge has a point marked 1 in. from the corner and a line ruled from this point to the inner corner. Remove the two triangular pieces marked and repeat the whole operation for the other side.

The two strengthening bars are 16 in. lengths of 2 in. × 1 in. batten (indicated in Fig. 3 by broken lines across the main three boards) to which the three boards are bolted. The boards and battens are drilled as indicated in Fig. 3 and the front batten is bolted in position with four coach bolts (see Fig. 4). Do not at this point tighten the nuts with the spanner – finger tight will do. *Make sure also that the bolts are a tight fit in the drilled holes.* The centre bolt on the back batten may also be fitted in position. The four outer bolts also hold the rear axles in position (see Figs. 7 and 8) but may at this point be fitted to hold the complete structure firmly. (*For positioning, check with the rear axle detail in Fig. 3*).

The steering board is a 19 in. length of $3\frac{3}{4}$ in. × $\frac{3}{4}$ in. timber, angled at each end to a depth of $1\frac{1}{4}$ in. from a point $3\frac{1}{4}$ in. from the centre of the front edge on each side. (See Fig. 3.) The $\frac{7}{16}$ in. centre hole is drilled and a corresponding hole drilled in the centre board. The four $\frac{1}{4}$ in. axle holes and the steering rope holes may also be drilled. (*For their positions see the front axle detail, Fig. 3.*).

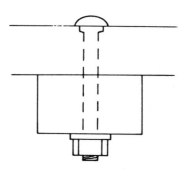

Fig. 4. Method of bolting front batten

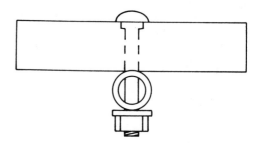

Fig. 5. Method of bolting rear axle

118

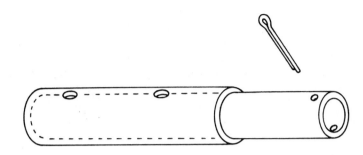

Fig. 6. Rear axle construction

The axles

If the axles are made and drilled before drilling the axle holes in the main structure, they can be used to mark the main structure axle holes and thus ensure that the assembly is correctly lined up.

The front axles can simply be two 6 in. lengths of $\frac{1}{2}$ in. diameter mild steel tubing. (If a manufactured axle is used the steering pivot is off-set to the front (as shown in Fig. 3) so that the axle can bridge the complete width of the steering board.) Drill a $\frac{1}{16}$ in. hole right through the axle $\frac{1}{4}$ in. from the outer end of each axle to take the split pins (see Fig. 6). Drill corresponding holes to line up with the holes in the steering board, making sure that the axles protrude 2 in. and assemble – once again only finger tight. Here 2 in. coach bolts will do, but there must be room for locking washers or locking nuts (see Fig. 5).

The back axles must be stronger and must protrude further to allow sufficient clearance between the wheels and the sides of the cart to prevent fingers from becoming trapped. Cut two 6 in. lengths of $\frac{1}{2}$ in. diameter tubing, as for the front axles, and two 4 in. lengths of steel tubing with an inside diameter of $\frac{1}{2}$ in. Hammer the two longer lengths of tubing into the shorter pieces, making sure that they reach the ends (Fig. 6). Drill two

$\frac{1}{4}$ in. holes through the double tubing, allowing the axles to protrude $2\frac{1}{2}$ in. Drill the holes for the split pins as for the front axles. Assemble finger tight with four $2\frac{1}{2}$ in. coach bolts (Figs. 7 and 8).

The axles must now be fitted with large washers with $\frac{1}{2}$ in. diameter centres before placing the wheels upon them, and a further large washer should be placed over each protruding axle before fitting the split pin (see Fig. 6). Ensure that there is free movement of the wheels on the axles and make sure there is not too much lateral play. If there is, use thicker washers or add further washers to take up the movement. Remove split-pins,

washers and wheels.

The steering stop block is a $6\frac{1}{2}$ in. length of timber 2 in. × 1 in. with the corners removed.

All the parts are now ready for final assembly. The steering board must be removed and a 3 in. diameter washer placed between the centre board and the steering board (Fig. 9). The nut and bolt can now be tightened with the spanner. *A lock-nut must be used.* Check that the steering moves easily but not loosely.

The front axle bolts are next tightened; the square portion under the domed head of each bolt must disappear into the

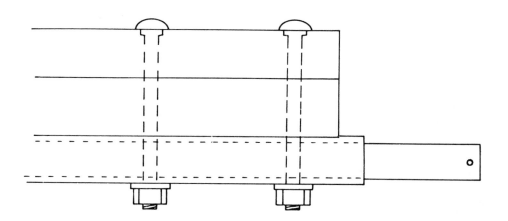

Fig. 7. Rear axle in position

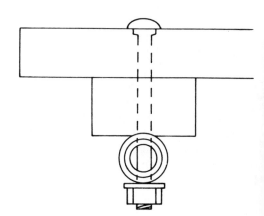

Fig. 8. Rear axle: section

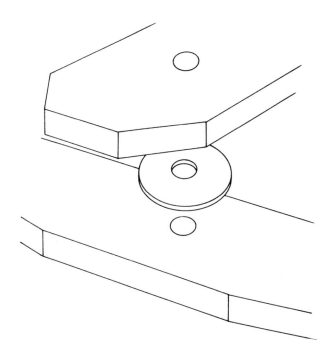

Fig. 9. Steering board and washer

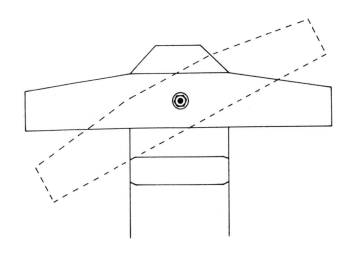

Fig. 10. Steering stop block

wood so that the underside of the domed head is flush with the wood. Do not overtighten. The nuts on the strengthening battens and the rear axle can also be tightened. Check that there is no relative movement between boards or axles. Do not at this point attach the wheels.

The steering stop block can now be glued and screwed to the underside of the centre board $1\frac{1}{2}$ in. from the rear edge of the steering board (Fig. 10).

121

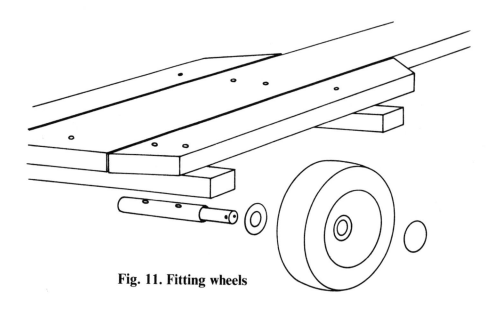

Fig. 11. Fitting wheels

The go-cart can now be sanded and painted. When it is dry, fit the wheels (Figs. 11 and 12), making sure that the split-pins are bent over properly and cannot come loose. If the wheels have hub caps these will hide the split-pins and washers; if not, make sure that there are no sharp protrusions.

All that is now needed to finish the go-cart is the steering rope. A 60 in. length of polypropylene or nylon rope inserted through the two holes in the steering board and knotted underneath is all that is required (Fig. 13). *Make sure that the knot is large enough to prevent it from being pulled through the hole.*

Should you wish to have a brake on the go-cart, this is simply made by bolting a 4 in. length of 2 in. × 1 in. batten to the underside of the right-hand (or, if you prefer, left-hand) seat-

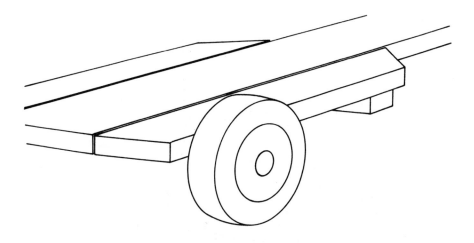

Fig. 12. Rear wheels in position

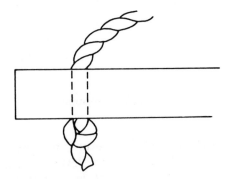

Fig. 13. Knot securing steering rope

123

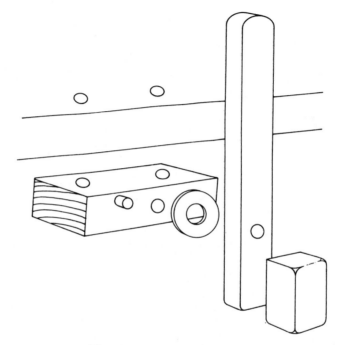

Fig. 14. Brake: components

board flush with the outer edge, and 1 in. forward of the rear axle support. Drill a hole through the centre of this 4 in. batten to take the brake lever bolt. The brake lever is an 8 in. length of $1\frac{1}{2}$ in. $\times$ $\frac{3}{4}$ in. batten with a 2 in. length of $1\frac{1}{2}$ in. $\times$ 1 in. wood glued and screwed to it as a brake block (Fig. 14). Round off the corners of the brake lever and drill a $\frac{1}{4}$ in. hole through the

lever $\frac{1}{2}$ in. above the brake block. Using a 4 in. coach bolt bolt the lever, with a washer between it and the support, to the brake support batten. *Do not overtighten.* To prevent the brake from rubbing the wheel while it is moving, a small tension spring and a 'stop-peg' must be fitted. A dome-headed screw protruding $\frac{1}{2}$ in. will make an admirable stop-peg.

The go-cart is now finished but a thorough check is advisable before 'carting'. Make sure that the following points are covered:

All nuts are tightened correctly.
Wheels are secure and move freely.
Steering bar moves freely and connects correctly with the steering stop when in the full lock position.
Steering rope is secure and will not pull out of the holes. If a brake is fitted make sure it operates properly and remains tensioned against the stop-peg.

These points should also be checked at frequent intervals when the go-cart is in use.

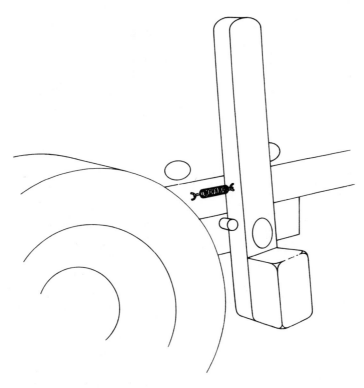

Fig. 15. Brake assembled

Climbing frame

TOOLS

Tenon saw
Try square
Brace and bit (or drill) and countersink bit
Screwdriver
Sandpaper
Paintbrushes

MATERIALS

The climbing frame is made almost entirely from equal lengths of 2 in. × 1 in. softwood batten glued and screwed or bolted together to form a box-like structure. Floors or platforms are cut from $\frac{3}{4}$ in. plywood, and if required wall panels can be cut from hardboard.

Although specified measurements are given, the following instructions can be used to build a garden climbing frame, merely by doubling the length of the battens and doubling the size of the platforms. Thicker and wider battens are then necessary; they should be not less than $2\frac{1}{2}$ in. × $1\frac{1}{4}$ in. If the platforms and the walls are likely to be left out in the garden, marine-grade plywood must be used. Ladders can be made using the frame uprights as ladder rails, with lengths of 1 in. diameter wooden dowel (or broomstick) or further lengths of batten as rungs.

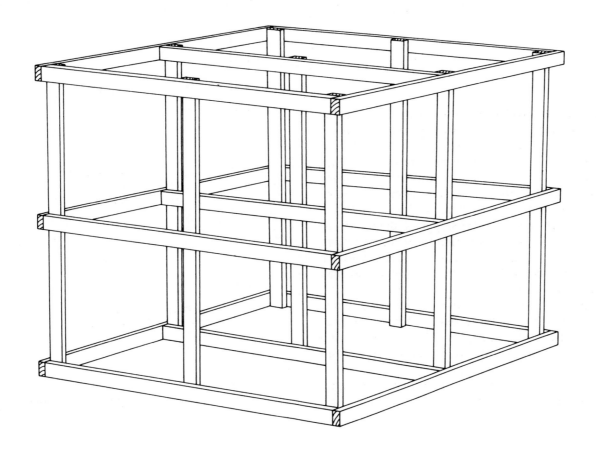

Fig. 1. The basic framework

The platforms and walls are not permanent parts of the main structure and can therefore be moved about to enable a wide variety of games.

METHOD

The frame

The basic frame is constructed from twenty-four 48 in. lengths of 2 in. × 1 in. softwood battens. As all twenty-four lengths are identical the framework can be of any size you wish, but crossrails and posts of 56 in. and longer must be at least $2\frac{1}{2}$ in. × $1\frac{1}{4}$ in. The simplest method of assembling the framework (Fig. 1) is by first making a single side comprising six battens (Fig. 2). The three crossmembers are glued and screwed to the three uprights (Fig. 3). Use two screws staggered diagonally at each fixing point (Fig. 4), making sure that the whole structure is perfectly square. *The centre upright and crossbar must be absolutely central* or there will be problems when the play platforms are being fitted. To prevent the crossmembers and uprights from splitting, first drill holes of half the screw diameters completely through the crossmembers, and two-thirds of the way through the uprights before inserting and tightening the screws. Use $1\frac{7}{8}$ in. countersunk screws and countersink *all* screwheads.

Make up two more identical frames, continually checking for squareness and correct positioning.

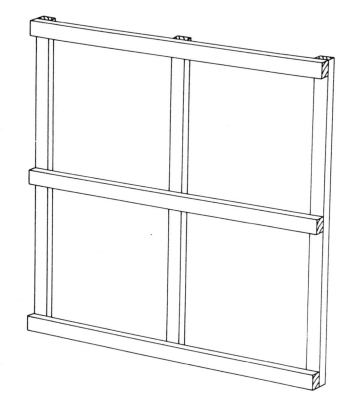

Fig. 2. Single side of frame

128

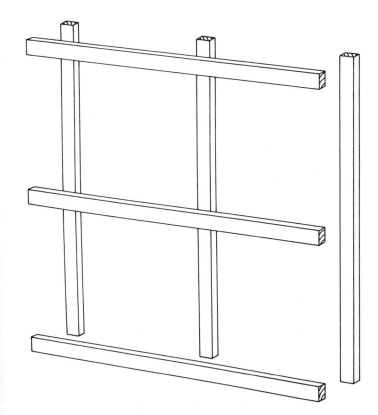

Fig. 3. Crossmembers and supports

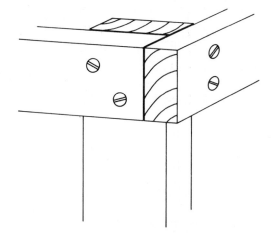

Fig. 4. Method of staggering screws at joints

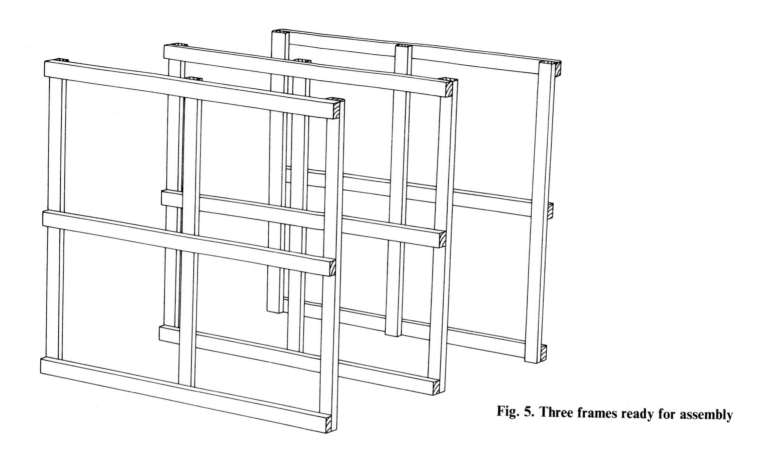

Fig. 5. Three frames ready for assembly

The three frames are then positioned with the crossmembers facing outward on the two outside frames (Fig. 5). The three frames are then glued and screwed together with six crossmembers (Fig. 6), once again using two screws at each fixing point (Fig. 4). *The screws must be positioned so that they enter the sides of the uprights not the end of the crossmembers.* Stagger the screws slightly diagonally, taking great care not to split the timber. The crossmembers are drilled through as

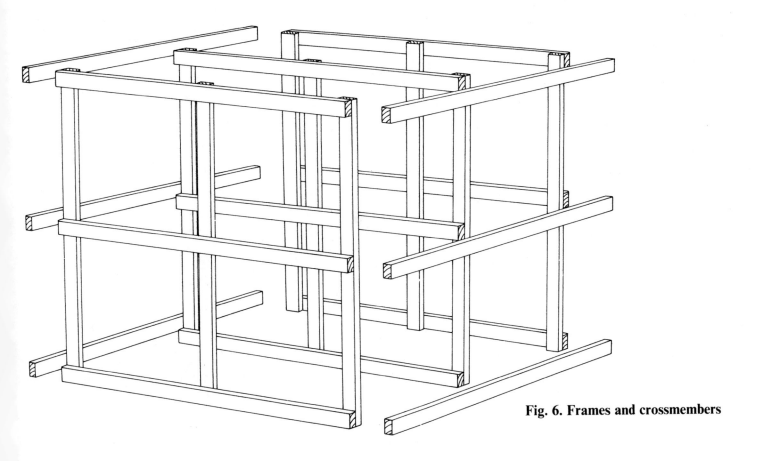

Fig. 6. Frames and crossmembers

before, the uprights to a depth of approximately $\frac{1}{2}$ in. and *all* screwheads countersunk.

The main structure is then complete and the floors can now be cut and fitted.

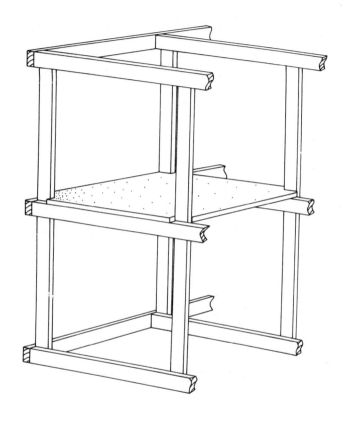

Fig. 7. Floor

The floors

The two floors (Fig. 7) are identical in size and shape (one is inverted) and are cut from $\frac{3}{4}$ in. plywood. If the climbing frame is to be used out of doors then marine-grade plywood must be used.

A simple method of finding the correct size and shape for the floors is to place the frame on a piece of cardboard approximately 26 in. square. With a pencil, mark round the corner of the frame base and mark the position of each of the four uprights. Draw a line from each of the rectangles formed by the uprights and the outer edges of the frame and you will have a shape as shown in Fig. 8. Cut this shape out with a craft knife and straight-edge, or with scissors, and check that the

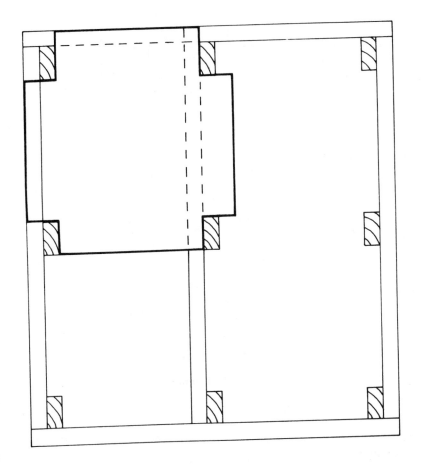

piece of cardboard fits easily into place on the centre crossmembers. If you have assembled the frame correctly the cardboard shape will be correct and can be used as a template for the two floors. If the frame has been assembled slightly out of square it will be a simple matter to rectify the cardboard template. If a piece of plywood had been cut undersize it would have been wasted.

N.B. The floors can only be fitted diagonally when both are in position but they are interchangeable to any of the four corner sections.

The floors may be screwed to the crossmembers if you wish or permanent floor sections can be made of lengths of the same batten that is used for the main structure.

Fig. 8. Floor: plan

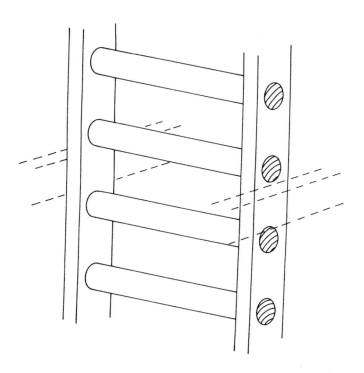

Fig. 9. Ladder

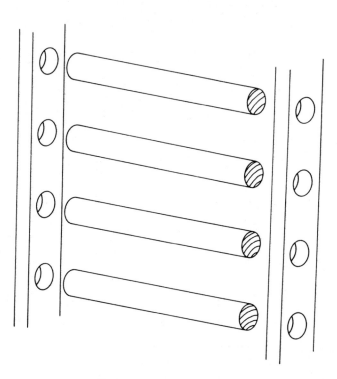

Fig. 10. Ladder: assembly

Ladders

A ladder to the floor is easily made by using two of the uprights as ladder rails. For rungs, either 1 in. wooden dowel or lengths of batten can be glued and screwed into position (Figs. 9 and 10). If dowel is used for the rungs, holes of 1 in. diameter must be drilled in the ladder rails with the rungs glued and pinned into position. The disadvantage of dowel rungs is that they can be inserted only into the wider surface of the uprights, whereas batten rungs can be screwed to the uprights in any position.

A separate ladder can be made using either method but it should **fit** firmly to the frame, especially if small children are to play upon it. A couple of locating brackets can easily be made to fit over the crossmembers of the frame and screwed to the ladder.

Wall panels

If required, wall panels can be cut from hardboard or plywood. Once again, use marine plywood if the climbing frame is to stay in the garden. Make the panels of a uniform size so that they can be interchangeable. A quarter of an end panel – to fit between the crossmembers – is an ideal size. A simple method of fixing is by hanging the panels on dome-headed screws left protruding just sufficiently for the panel to slide on to them (Fig. 11). Make sure that the screws do not protrude in such a way as to be dangerous. Another method of fixing the panels is by means of turnbuttons, which are obtainable at most hardware shops.

PAINTING AND FINISHING

Sand the climbing frame smooth and slightly round off all corners that may injure small children. Varnish or paint to your choice. The floor panels and wall panels can be painted in a variety of bright colours, or if you prefer they can be varnished. The climbing frame is now ready.

MAINTENANCE

It is advisable to check the framework and panels regularly for damage or loosening of the joints. It is far better to tighten a screw or two or remove a few splinters from the climbing frame than to have to deal with injuries to fingers or knees.

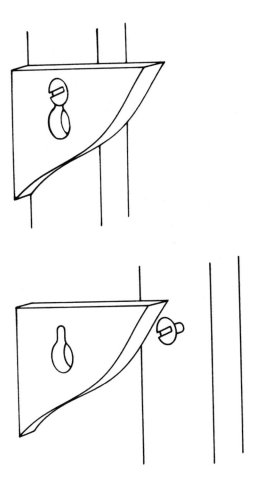

Fig. 11. Method of fixing panels

REINFORCEMENT

Should the climbing frame appear to loosen slightly after a time and the three separate frames (Fig. 5) move slightly within the joining six crossmembers, simple 'tie blocks' can be made from 6 in. × 6 in. blocks of softwood 1 in. thick cut diagonally in half to form two right-angled triangles. The tie blocks must be firmly glued and screwed into position between the three frames and the six crossmembers as shown in Fig. 12. The end grain of the tie blocks must run at right-angles to the deeply countersunk screws that enter the uprights of the three frames.

A tie block at each corner of the three frames (12 blocks in all) should be sufficient, but blocks may also be fixed to the centre frame if required.

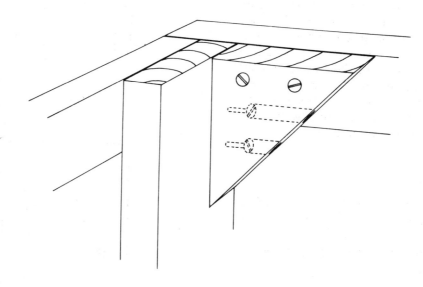

Fig. 12. Tie blocks for reinforcement

Two-seater rocker and playboat

TOOLS

Panel saw
Tenon saw
Brace and bit (or hand drill)
$\frac{1}{4}$ in. and 1 in. chisels and mallet
Screwdriver
Hammer
Rasp
Sandpaper
Paintbrushes

MATERIALS

The rocker/playboat (Fig. 1) is made almost entirely from $\frac{1}{2}$ in. plywood with 1 in. × $\frac{7}{8}$ in. batten for the seat supports. A length of 1 in. diameter dowel forms the handrail. (This may be omitted if the toy is intended only as a playboat.) A pair of 'oars' to complete the playboat are made from two lengths of $\frac{5}{8}$ in. diameter dowel and two pieces of $\frac{1}{8}$ in. hardboard.

METHOD

The two sides, seat backs and seats are cut from $\frac{1}{2}$ in. plywood; 1 in. × $\frac{7}{8}$ in. softwood battens form the seat supports while also being the means by which the sides are held in position (Fig. 2).

It may be found easier to cut out the two sides if the plywood is sawn into 36 in. × 16 in. rectangles before cutting it to shape. The grid marked on the side plan (Fig. 3) represents 6 in. squares. To transfer the shape of one side draw a grid of 6 in. squares on one of the pieces of plywood. On this grid mark with dots each point where a line of the drawing crosses the lines of the grid. Join up the dots, taking care to follow the curves of the plan, to get your plan at full size. Repeat the whole operation for the other side and carefully cut them both out. The curves can easily be sawn with the tenon saw by cutting away straight sections at different angles around the outside of the marked shape and finishing off with the rasp and sandpaper. Take great care that both ends of each side are identical and that both rocker curves are the same or the rocker/playboat will not rock properly.

The seat backs are two 14 in. × 10 in. pieces of plywood. The two seats are 14 in. × 9 in. (The seat depth can be increased to 10 in. if leg room for bigger children is not a consideration.) Make sure that the corners and edges are square or the rocker/playboat will not assemble firmly and properly.

The battens are of 1 in. × $\frac{7}{8}$ in. softwood of the same length as the seat backs and seats (Fig. 3). Screw the seats and seat backs on to the $\frac{7}{8}$ in. surface of the battens, making sure that the battens line up perfectly and squarely with the outer edges of the plywood panels. The screw heads must be countersunk and

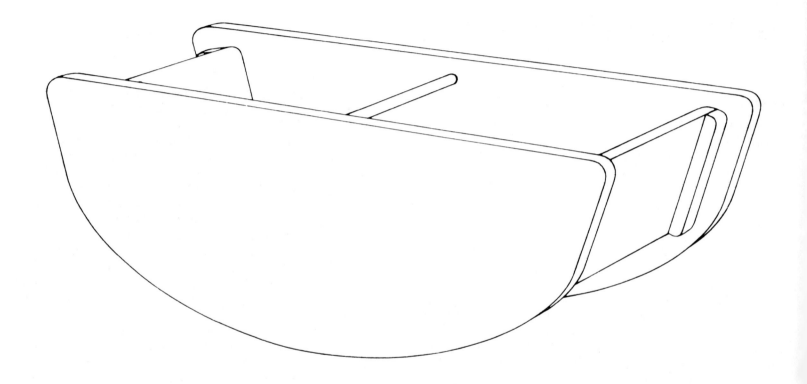

Fig. 1. The rocker/playboat

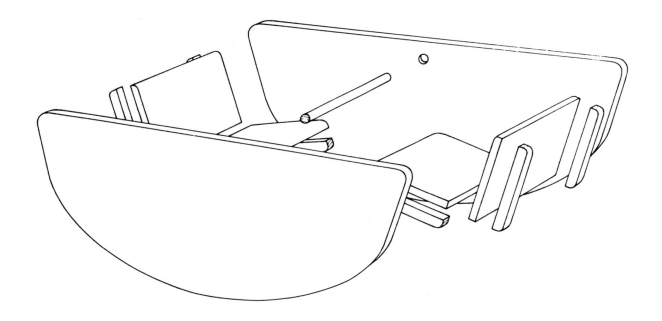

Fig. 2. The rocker/playboat: components

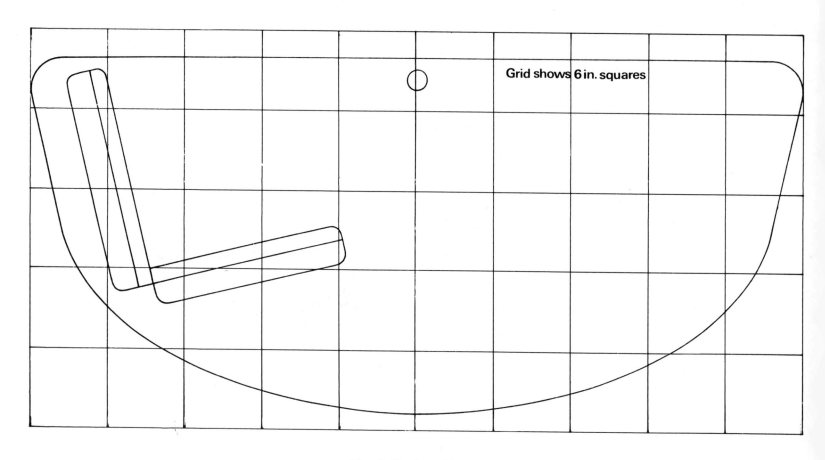

Grid shows 6 in. squares

Fig. 3. Rocker sides

filled. Round off the batten ends and the forward edges of the seat and seat back and sand them smooth (Fig. 4). The handrail is a length of 1 in. dowel and can be fitted in various ways. The simplest is a socket $\frac{1}{4}$ in. deep drilled or chiselled into the inside surface of each of the rocker/playboat sides (Fig. 5a) in the position indicated in the side view (Fig. 3). If this method is used, a 14$\frac{1}{2}$ in. length of dowel will be necessary. If preferred, the 'socket' holes can be drilled through small pieces of plywood and these then fixed into position (Fig. 5b). This method requires a 14 in. length of dowel. Yet another way of fixing the handrail is by drilling a $\frac{1}{2}$ in. hole through the rocker/playboat side and a further $\frac{1}{2}$ in. hole, 1 in. deep, centrally in each end of the handrail dowel. A 1$\frac{1}{2}$ in. length of $\frac{1}{2}$ in. dowel can then be glued into each end of the handrail and inserted into the corresponding holes in the sides (Fig. 5c).

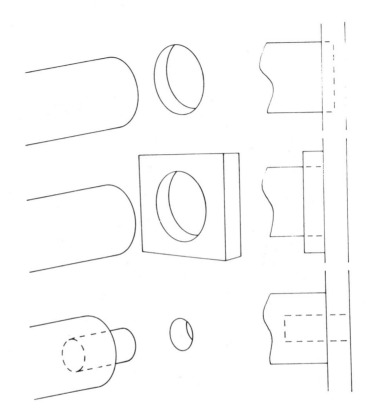

Fig. 5. Fitting the handrail

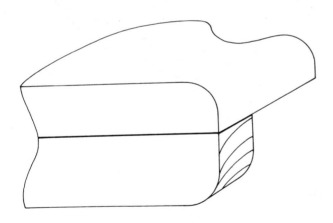

Fig. 4. Rounded seat edges and battens

141

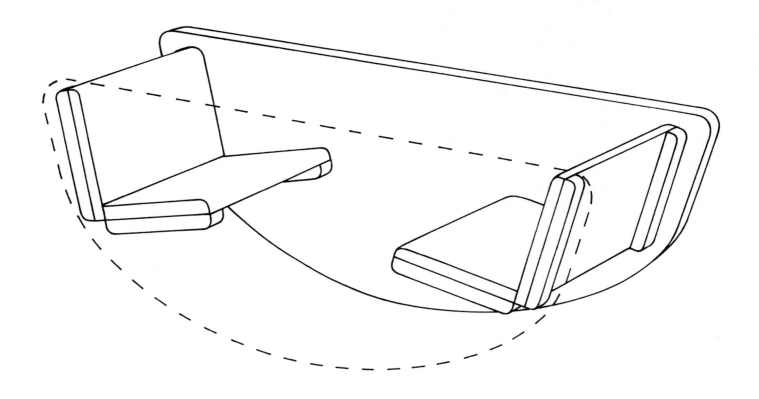

Fig. 6. Rocker assembly

If preferred, all the parts of the rocker/playboat can be painted before assembly, but care must be taken that the painted surfaces are completely dry before being assembled.

The exact positions of the seats and seat backs are shown in the side view (Fig. 3). It will be found helpful to place the pieces into position with one side laid flat and to pencil lightly round the battens. Holes can then be drilled through the side within the pencilled areas for the side assembly screws. Take care not to foul any of the screws holding the seats or seat backs to the battens.

Repeat the whole operation for the other side. The seats and the seat backs can now be screwed to one side (Fig. 6). The screws, which must be domed, are inserted from the outside of the rocker/playboat side. The remaining side may now be fixed in position *but do not forget to insert the handrail first* and check that the two sides are in line with one another and that the whole structure rocks evenly. The rocker/playboat is now complete. If you have not painted it before assembly it can now be painted and finished to your choice.

PLAYBOAT 'OARS'

A pair of oars (Fig. 7) is all that is needed to convert the rocker to a playboat. They are easily made from $\frac{5}{8}$ in. diameter dowel and $\frac{1}{8}$ in. hardboard. The oars are made in two parts: (a) the handle and (b) the blade (Fig. 8).

The handle is a 20 in. length of $\frac{5}{8}$ in. diameter wooden dowel rounded at each end, with the bottom 5 in. cut flat on one side to allow it to be firmly fixed to the blade.

To cut the flat area on the handle, first make a number of saw-cuts with the tenon saw to a depth of approximately $\frac{1}{8}$ in. The furthest saw-cut up the handle should be 5 in. from the bottom end (Fig. 9). The area below this first cut is then

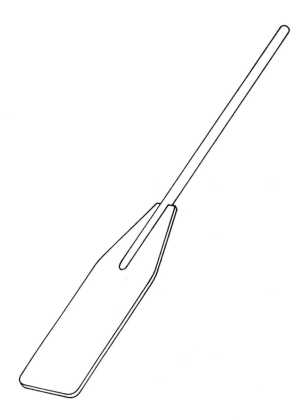

Fig. 7. Oar for playboat

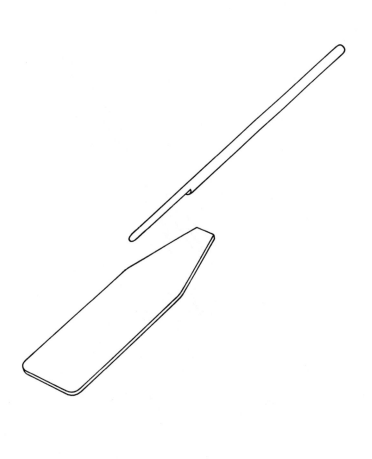

Fig. 8. Oar: components

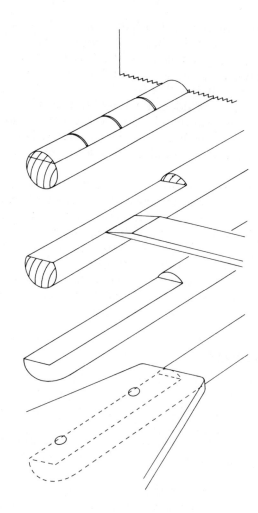

Fig. 9. Cutting the flat on the oar handle

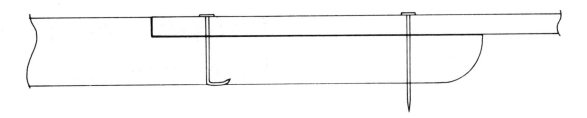

Fig. 10. Method of nailing oar blade to handle

removed with the large chisel, taking great care not to remove too much of the dowel. The resulting flat area can now be sanded smooth. Check that it is indeed flat. Repeat the whole procedure for the second oar. The blade of the oar is a 15 in. × 4½ in. rectangle of ⅛ in. hardboard tapered centrally to 1¼ in. wide at the top from a point each side of the rectangle 8 in. from the bottom. The corners are then rounded off and the blade is glued and pinned to the handle. Repeat for the seond oar.

Use thin, large-headed 1 in. nails so that the protruding ends can be hammered over flush with the surface of the handle (Fig. 10). The nails must be hammered through the hardboard not into it. Take care not to split the oar handles and make sure that the pointed ends are well embedded in the handles. The oars may now be painted or varnished.

If the rocker/playboat is going to be used as a playboat the handrail may be omitted and two 'U'-shaped notches cut centrally in the upper edges of the playboat sides. The 'U'-shaped notches will make admirable rowlocks.

The rocker/playboat described and illustrated is for small children, but a larger version can easily be made.

N.B. The playboat and oars are only for 'make-believe' boating and are under no circumstances to be used anywhere but indoors or in the garden on dry land.

Baby-walker and brick trolley

TOOLS

Tenon saw
Fretsaw or coping saw
Try square
Brace and bit or drill
Chisel and mallet
Pair of compasses, or jar or tin lid 4 in. to $4\frac{1}{2}$ in. diameter
Hammer
Screwdriver
Sandpaper
Paintbrushes

MATERIALS

The baby walker/brick trolley basic frame is cut from $2\frac{3}{4}$ in. × $\frac{3}{4}$ in. timber with hardboard for the base. The wheels are cut from $\frac{3}{4}$ in. plywood or can be made from several thicknesses of thinner plywood glued together. The axles and the handlebar are of $\frac{3}{4}$ in. dowel with the handle struts cut from $1\frac{1}{4}$ in. × $\frac{3}{8}$ in. batten. The complete handle is made so that removal of it from the basic frame, the simple addition of a screw eye at one end, and a length of cord converts the baby walker into a brick trolley. The bricks are very easily made, from scraps of timber and dowel. In addition, you will need panel pins, screws and adhesive.

Fig. 1. The baby walker/brick trolley

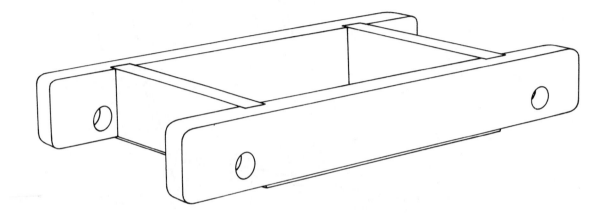

Fig. 2. Brick box frame

METHOD

The brick box basic frame (Fig. 2) is cut from $2\frac{3}{4}$ in. $\times$ $\frac{3}{4}$ in. timber with the ends fixed to the sides by means of a through-housing joint (Fig. 3). The side pieces are 18 in. long with the ends rounded off at the corners. The end pieces are 8 in. long and are left square at the ends. It is extremely important to use a try square: all cut ends and corners must be perfectly square.

$2\frac{1}{4}$ in. from each end of the side pieces, mark on one side a line running *squarely* across the timber with a further line $\frac{3}{4}$ in. towards the centre. With the tenon saw cut into the timber $\frac{1}{4}$ in. deep on each of the drawn lines, taking great care to keep the saw upright; ensure that the saw-cut is $\frac{1}{4}$ in. deep along the whole of its length (Fig. 4a). The sections between the saw-cuts

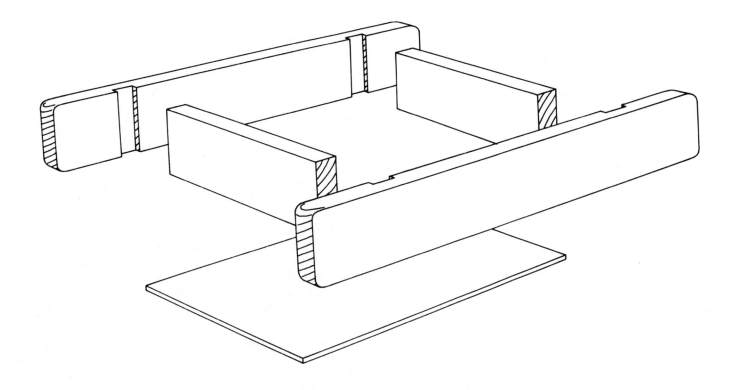

Fig. 3. Brick box frame: components

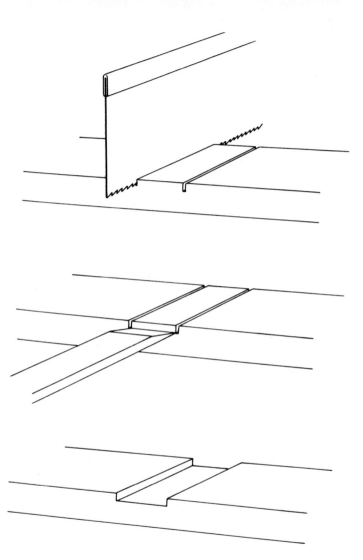

Fig. 4. Cutting grooves for joints in frame

are now removed with a chisel and mallet (Fig. 4b) and the resulting groove is cleaned up (Fig. 4c). Do not make the grooves too wide: the ends of the end pieces of the basic frame must fit firmly and squarely within them.

The axle holes can now be drilled. Mark a point $\frac{5}{8}$ in. from the outer edge of each groove, $\frac{3}{4}$ in. from the bottom edge of each of the side pieces, and drill the four $\frac{7}{8}$ in. diameter axle holes. *Check that the $\frac{3}{4}$ in. dowel rotates easily within them and does not catch at all.*

Sand the four pieces smooth and assemble (Fig. 5). The joints *must* be glued and pinned. There is no need to punch the nail heads below the surface and fill the holes, since they are hidden behind the wheels.

The bottom or base of the unit is simply a 13 in. × $8\frac{3}{4}$ in. rectangle of hardboard. Do not at this point fix it to the brick box basic frame.

The wheels are cut from $\frac{3}{4}$ in. plywood or from two or three thicknesses of thinner plywood glued together to make up $\frac{3}{4}$ in. A couple of 'G'-clamps with some waste plywood or hardboard to protect the wheel plywood will help to hold the layers together while the adhesive is drying. If you have no clamps, anything heavy, such as a pile of old books or magazines, will do just as well.

Use the compasses to mark out four circles $4\frac{1}{4}$ in. in diameter, or draw round a tin or jar of approximately the same diameter. It is advisable to drill the axle holes before cutting the wheels out, making absolutely sure that the holes are central. The holes must be small enough for the axle dowel to be really tight fit. A sawing block which will simplify the wheel-cutting operation can easily be made from an odd piece of plywood, as described on p. 9. Screwed or clamped to the work-bench it will provide an excellent base upon which to cut out the wheels with a fretsaw or coping saw. The method of using a fretsaw is described on p. 8.

Sand all four wheels smooth and round off the outer edges to prevent splitting. The axles are simply two 11 in. lengths of $\frac{3}{4}$ in. dowel cut squarely and smooth at each end so they fit flush with the outer surfaces of the wheels.

The handle is a $9\frac{3}{4}$ in. length of $\frac{3}{4}$ in. dowel supported by two 20 in. lengths of $1\frac{1}{4}$ in. × $\frac{3}{8}$ in. battens rounded at each end (see also Fig. 10). At the top ends of the two battens drill a hole small enough for the handle dowel to be a really tight fit (Fig. 6). At the bottom ends drill two small holes to prevent the fixing screws from splitting the battens. The dowel is then glued and pinned into the support battens. Lay the complete structure on a flat surface to ensure that the battens are parallel and in an identical position.

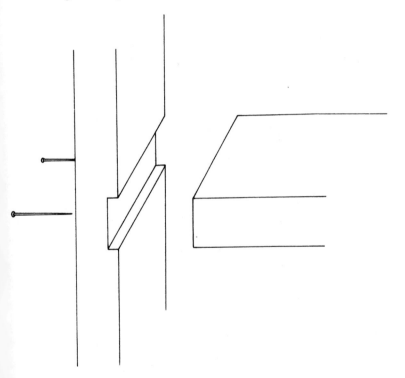

Fig. 5. Assembling the frame

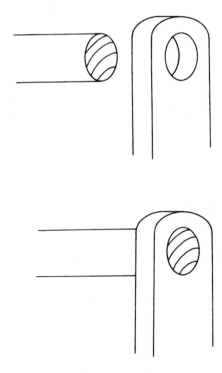

Fig. 6. Fitting dowel to battens

151

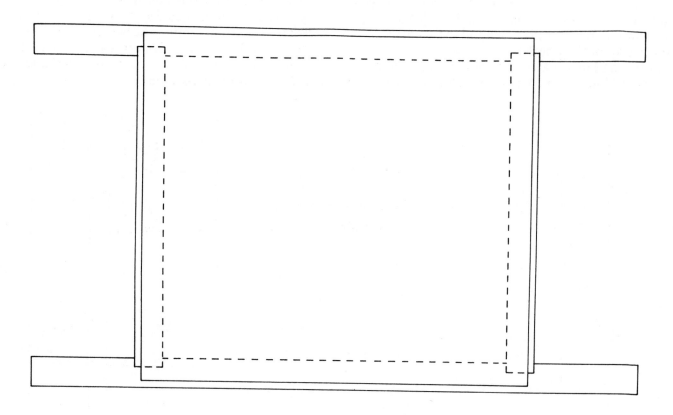

Fig. 7. Fitting base of brick box

152

All the parts of the baby walker are now ready for painting prior to assembly. *Remember to use non-toxic paints.* The bottom of the brick box can be of contrasting colour to the sides, perhaps matching the handles, and the wheels yet another contrasting colour. When the parts are perfectly dry they can be assembled.

The base (painted surface uppermost) must be screwed to the underside of the brick box so that it is positioned squarely and centrally upon the four edges of the sides (Fig. 7). The axles are then inserted through the axle holes in the main frame. Before gluing the wheels to the axles, spacer washers must be added to ensure free movement of the wheels without friction against the sides of the brick box (Figs. 8 and 9). These can easily be made from hardboard, plywood or even linoleum. The bottom end of each handle batten is then screwed to the outer sides of the brick box approximately $3\frac{1}{2}$ in. forward of the rear wheels. The angle of the handle must be such that the handlebar is slightly forward of the rear axle (Fig. 10). *This is extremely important if the baby walker is to be of help to a child learning to walk.* The screws holding the handle battens to the brick box can be

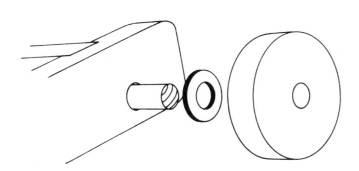

Fig. 8. Assembling wheels and axles

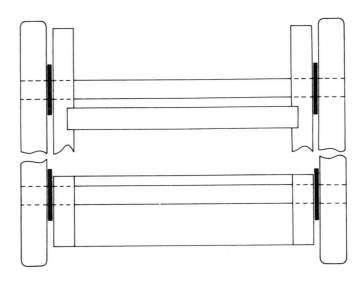

Fig. 9. Frame, wheels, axles and washers

covered by small plastic caps (obtainable at most hardware and do-it-yourself stores). The axles may now be painted or varnished. Take great care not to allow any paint or varnish to enter the axle holes.

BRICKS

Bricks can be made very cheaply and easily from odd scraps of wood. They can, for example, be cut from lengths of 1¾ in. square, ⅞ in. square, 1¾ in. × ¾ in. batten and 1 in. diameter dowel (Fig. 11). Arches can be made from 3 in. lengths of the timber left over from making the basic frame of the baby walker/brick trolley (Fig. 12).

Before painting the bricks ensure that all edges and corners

Fig. 10. Correct position for handlebar

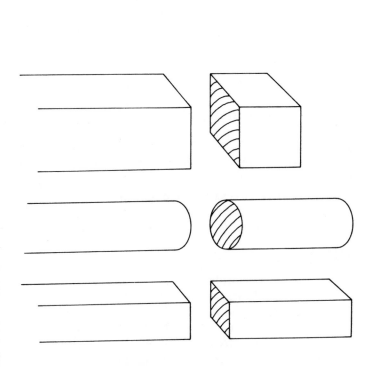

Fig. 11. Cutting bricks

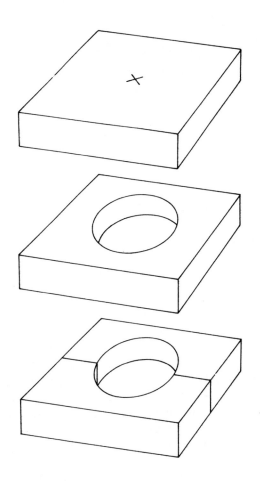

Fig. 12. Cutting arches

are rounded and that all surfaces are perfectly smooth. *Use non-toxic paints* and vary the colours as much as possible. Wood dyes may be used if preferred.

Nursery slide

TOOLS

Tenon saw
Try square
Brace and bit (or drill), countersink bit, $\frac{15}{16}$ in. holesaw or wood bit
$\frac{3}{4}$ in. chisel and mallet
Screwdriver
Hammer
Sandpaper
Paintbrushes

MATERIALS

The framework of the slide and the ladder rails are made from $1\frac{1}{2}$ in. × 1 in. and 2 in. × 1 in. softwood batten. The ladder rungs are equal lengths of 1 in. diameter wooden dowel (or broomstick) with $\frac{3}{8}$ in. plywood as the slide base. The slide and ladder are joined by a 16 in. piano hinge.

Although specified measurements are given, the building instructions can be used to build a much larger slide, merely by increasing the sizes (except of course the slide width) by half, or even by doubling them. Thicker and wider battens and $\frac{1}{2}$ in. plywood are then necessary. If the dimensions are increased throughout by one-half, 2 in. × $1\frac{1}{4}$ in. batten should be used instead of $1\frac{1}{2}$ in. × 1 in. and $2\frac{1}{4}$ in. × $1\frac{1}{4}$ in., instead of 2 in. × 1 in. If the dimensions are doubled throughout, $2\frac{1}{2}$ in. × $1\frac{1}{4}$ in. batten should be used in place of $1\frac{1}{2}$ in. × 1 in. and $2\frac{1}{2}$ in. × $1\frac{1}{4}$ in. in place of 2 in. × 1 in. If larger children are to play on the slide the ladder rungs must be of thicker diameter dowel; or further lengths of softwood batten may be used, glued and screwed to the outer edges of the ladder rails as ladder rungs. If the slide is likely to be left out in the garden marine-grade plywood must be used.

METHOD

The slide (Fig. 1) is simply a 16 in. × 48 in. piece of $\frac{3}{8}$ in. plywood with two 48 in. lengths of $1\frac{1}{2}$ in. × 1 in. softwood batten glued and screwed flush to the outer upper edges (Fig. 2). The screws must be through the plywood from the underside. *All screwheads must be countersunk* and may be filled if required. If higher sides are required, 2 in. × 1 in. batten may be used.

A 16 in. length of 2 in. × 1 in. batten is glued and screwed to the underside of the top end of the slide to take the piano hinge, which is also screwed to a similar batten on the underside of the ladder rails (Fig. 3). The upper edges and the bottom end of the slide side battens and the underside edge of the plywood are rounded off and sanded smooth so that small fingers do not get damaged while sliding. Do not round off the top end of the slide side battens; they must form a straight and square

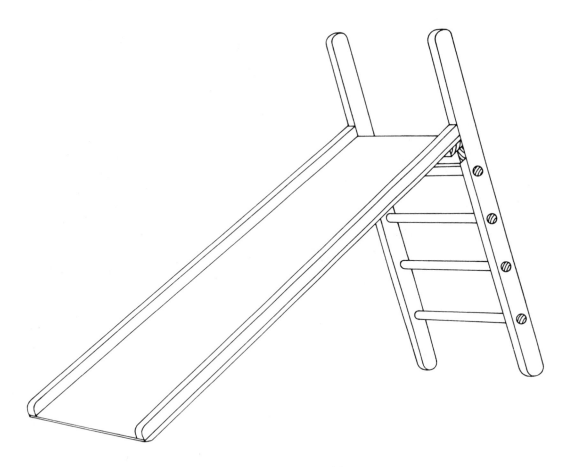

Fig. 1. The slide

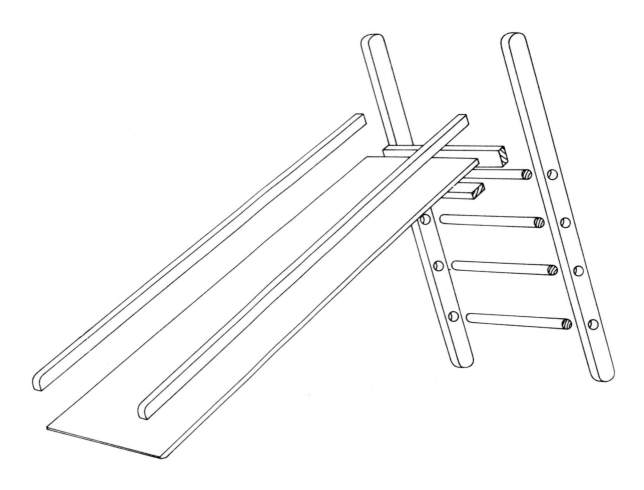

Fig. 2. Slide: components

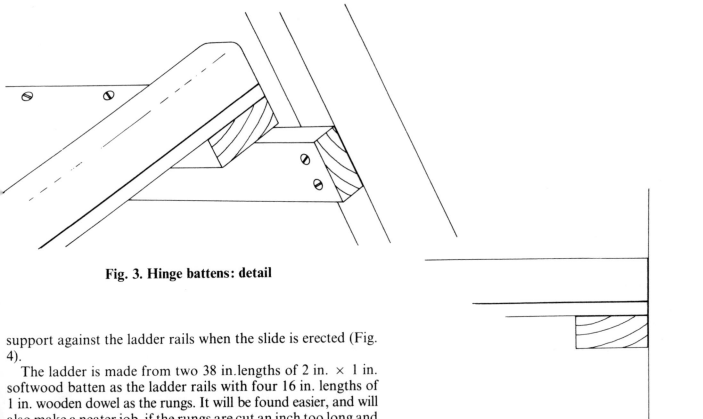

Fig. 3. Hinge battens: detail

Fig. 4. Positions for side battens and ladder rails (slide erected)

support against the ladder rails when the slide is erected (Fig. 4).

The ladder is made from two 38 in. lengths of 2 in. × 1 in. softwood batten as the ladder rails with four 16 in. lengths of 1 in. wooden dowel as the rungs. It will be found easier, and will also make a neater job, if the rungs are cut an inch too long and sawn off flush with the outer sides of the ladder rails after being glued and pinned into position. To drill the holes in the ladder rails, first mark a central point in the wider surface of one rail 6 in. from the bottom end; then mark a further three points each 6 in. apart. Drill a $\frac{15}{16}$ in. diameter hole at each of these four points through the ladder rail batten. Take great care not to

159

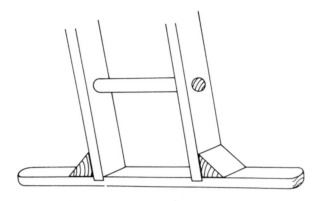

Fig. 5. Stabiliser

split the batten; drill halfway through from one side, then turn the batten over and drill from the other. Do not make the holes too large for the rungs – they must be a tight fit when the ladder is finally assembled. Repeat the whole operation for the other ladder rail and round off the top ends of both rails. Glue and pin the rungs in position (Fig. 2), cut them flush and sand smooth. If the nursery slide is intended only for very small children and is considered stable enough not to fall over sideways while being used, the bottom ends of the rails may also be rounded off. If, however, you feel that extra stability is necessary a stabiliser bar may be fitted (Fig. 5).

Cut a 30 in. length of 2 in. × 1 in. batten and round off each end. On the upper 2 in. surface, centrally mark two 1 in. wide slots 14 in. apart. Using the tenon saw cut to a depth of $\frac{1}{2}$ in. *on the waste side of the slot lines* (Fig. 6a). The waste is then removed with the chisel and mallet (Fig. 6b) and the two slots are cleaned out squarely (Fig. 6c). Check that the ladder rails fit

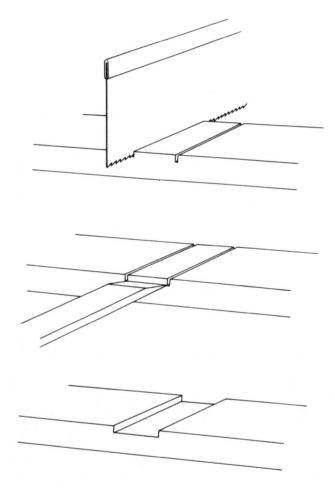

Fig. 6. Cutting slots in stabiliser bar

firmly and squarely into the slots but do not at this point fix them into position; the bottom ends of the ladder rails must be cut at the correct angle, which is more easily and correctly marked when the assembled slide is standing erect.

The ladder support bar is a 16 in. length of 2 in. × 1 in. batten glued and screwed squarely across the underside of the ladder rails 25 in. from the bottom (Figs. 2 and 3).

The slide and ladder can now be assembled by means of a 15–16 in. length of piano hinge screwed to the two support bars (Figs. 3 and 7). If a suitable length of hinge cannot be easily obtained, three or four smaller hinges may be used; but make sure that they are large enough and – above all – strong enough. Do not completely fix all the screws into position until you have checked that the two structures fit together firmly and squarely

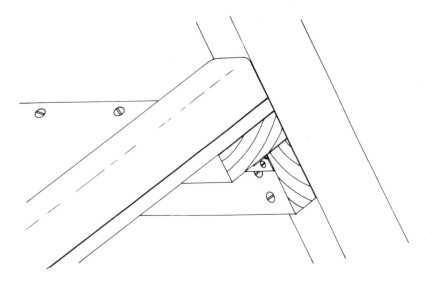

Fig. 7. Hinge detail

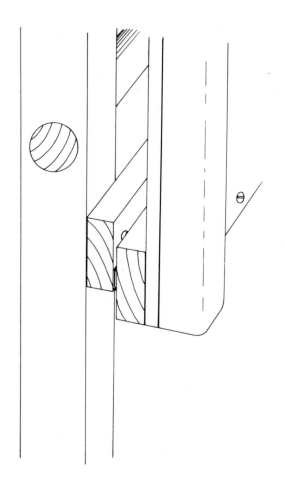

and fold flat properly (Fig. 8). The nursery slide can now be stood upright.

If the stabiliser bar is to be fitted, lay the bar flat on the surface on which the slide is standing, against the side of one of the ladder rails. Mark a pencil line across the rail along the upper surface of the stabiliser bar (Fig. 9). The section below the line is then removed. Repeat the whole operation for the other rail. Cut two right-angled triangular wedges from scrap softwood batten and glue and screw the stabiliser bar into position (Figs. 5 and 10). The slide is now ready to paint or varnish.

Fig. 8. Hinge detail (slide folded)

162

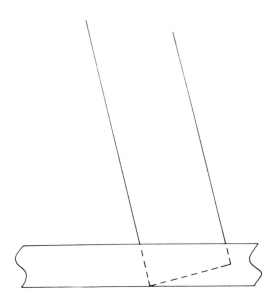

Fig. 9. Marking rails for fitting stabiliser

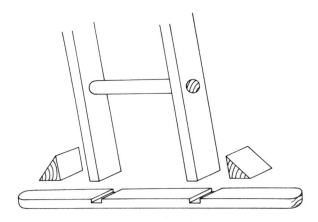

Fig. 10. Stabiliser bar and wedges

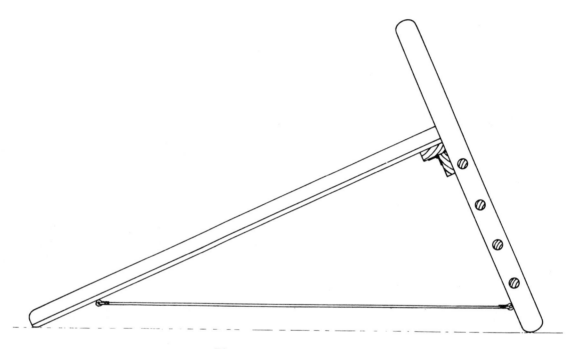

Fig. 11. Spreader cords

If you wish to strengthen the slide further, two spreader cords may be fitted (Fig. 11). From $1\frac{1}{2}$ in. eye-bolts and two 60 in. lengths of plastic-covered steel cable (the type that is used for clothes-line) will be needed. The reason for using steel cable is that it will not stretch and 'spring' the piano hinge and will also still allow the slide to be folded up and stored away when not in use. To fix the eye-bolts in position, first drill a hole, of large enough diameter to accommodate the eye-bolt nut, $\frac{1}{2}$ in.

deep centrally in the upper edge of one of the slide side battens 5 in. from the bottom end of the batten. Through the centre of this hole drill a further hole, large enough for the shank of the eye-bolt, right through the batten and plywood (Fig. 12a, b). Insert a nut into the upper hole, and pushing an eye-bolt through from the underside tighten the nut (Fig. 12c). Repeat the complete operation for the other slide side batten. Exactly, the same method is used for inserting the eye-bolts through the

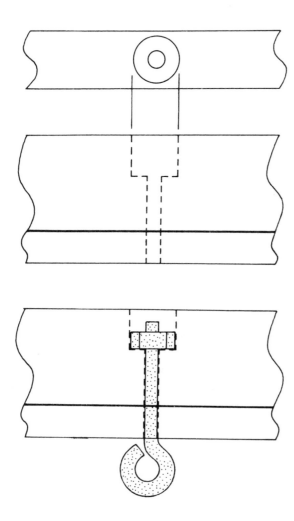

Fig. 12. Fixing eye-bolts

ladder rails. The holes are drilled centrally through from the outside edges of the ladder rails at the same height as the slide batten eye-bolt holes (measure from the surface on which the slide is standing), as shown in Fig. 11. The holes are then filled with cellulose filler if the slide is to be painted, or with plastic wood if the slide is to be varnished. Allow to dry and sand smooth. Paint or varnish to finish.

The cords must now be securely knotted, taking great care that each is of equal length and stretched taut when the slide is erect. The knots must not slip or loosen and must be tied and bound as shown in Fig. 13.

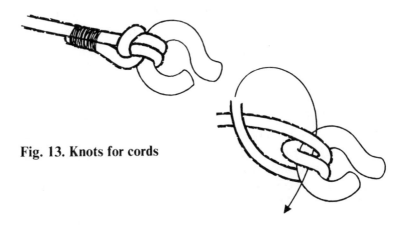

Fig. 13. Knots for cords

MAINTENANCE

Check the framework at frequent intervals and make sure that all joints are secure. Check at the same time that the cords are not frayed and the knots are secure. The surface of the slide should be examined for splinters.

Baby (nursery) swing

TOOLS

Tenon saw
Try square
Brace and $\frac{1}{4}$ in. bit (or drill) and $\frac{7}{8}$ in. hole saw or flat bit
Screwdriver
Sandpaper
Paintbrushes

MATERIALS

The baby-swing is made from two structures: (a) the frame (Fig. 1) and (b) the seat (Fig. 9). The frame 'legs' are made from $1\frac{1}{2}$ in. $\times$ $\frac{7}{8}$ in. timber with $\frac{3}{8}$ in. plywood corner strengtheners. The swing support bar, which also forms the top crossbar of the frame, is of 3 in. $\times$ 1 in. timber. The legs of the frame are attached to the swing support bar by $1\frac{1}{4}$ in. steel hinges and held in position by a spacer block of $\frac{3}{4}$ in. plywood, to which the legs are bolted by eight 2 in. screw-headed machine nuts and bolts.

The seat base is a 14 in. $\times$ 12 in. rectangle of $\frac{1}{2}$ in. plywood with four sides of $\frac{7}{8}$ in. $\times$ $\frac{5}{8}$ in. slats with $\frac{7}{8}$ in. dowel spacers threaded on to the swing support ropes.

The support ropes are looped through two shackles which are attached to two $3\frac{1}{2}$ in. eye-bolts in the swing support bar.

METHOD

The frame

The frame can best be described as two U-shaped legs hinged to a top crossbar (Fig. 2). The uprights are 70 in. long. The 48 in. bottom crosspieces are held in position with half-lap joints (Fig. 3a). The actual angles of the corners can be taken from the corner strengthener template (Fig. 4). The half-lap joints are glued and pinned (Fig. 3b). The corner strengtheners are cut from $\frac{3}{8}$ in. plywood (Fig. 4) and are glued and screwed into position with 1 in. dome-headed screws (Fig. 3c). The rounding-off of the corners can be done either before or after fixing the strengtheners. The swing support bar is a 20 in. length of 3 in. $\times$ 1 in. timber with two $\frac{1}{4}$ in. diameter holes drilled through it to take the $3\frac{1}{2}$ in. long eye-bolts which support the swing. The holes are drilled centrally in the upper surface, 3 in. from each end of the support bar. Make sure that the drill emerges centrally in the same position in the bottom surface (Fig. 8). The 'U' frame on one side can now be positioned on the swing support bar and the ends sawn off at the correct angle.

The angle of the hinge ends of the frame must run parallel with the swing support bar (Fig. 5) or the frame will not fold flat for storage. Take great care that the hinges are positioned

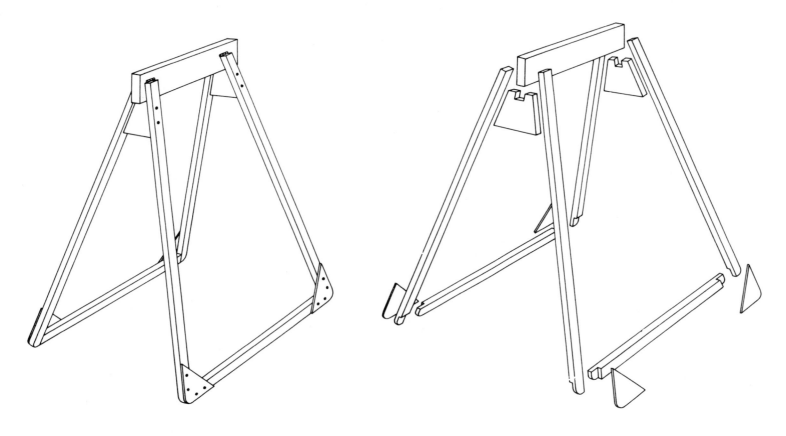

Fig. 1. The frame   **Fig. 2. Frame: components**

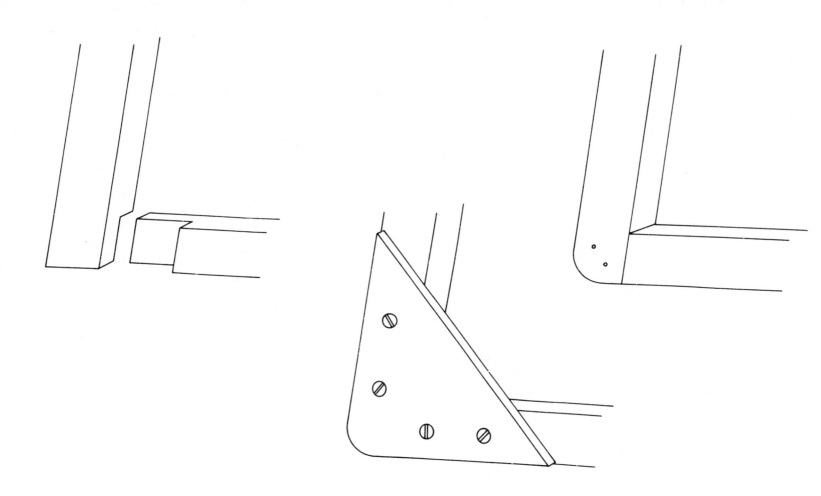

Fig. 3. Joints for frame crosspieces

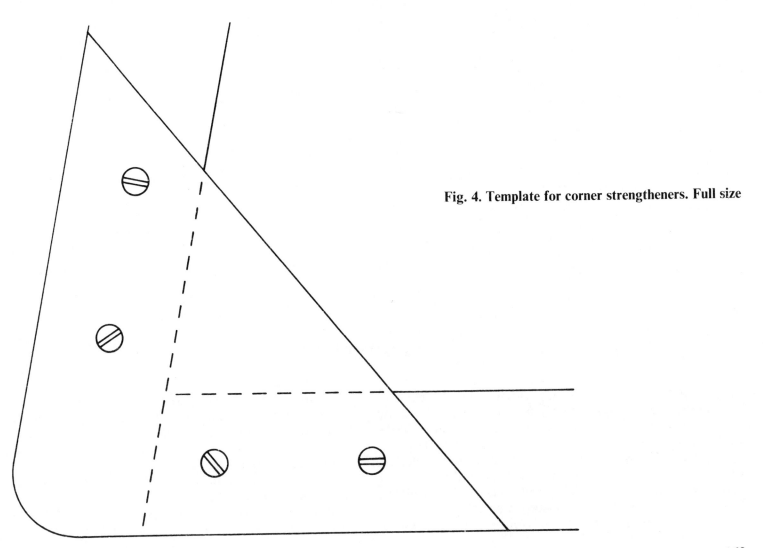

Fig. 4. Template for corner strengtheners. Full size

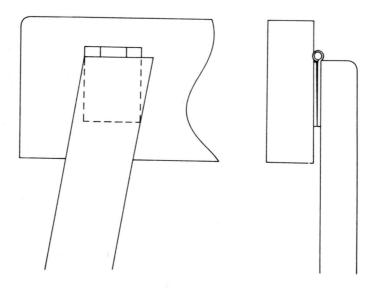

Fig. 5. Frame hinges

squarely and centrally on the support bar and that the screws holding the frame uprights do not split the timber. Be careful also not to split the swing support bar and make sure that the screws of one side of the bar do not foul the screws on the other. The 'U' frame on one side can be slightly offset or, if preferred, $\frac{1}{2}$ in.–1 in. narrower in width. On no account must screws less than 1 in. long be used. Always drill holes of approximately half the diameter of the screws before assembling.

The spacer blocks are made from $\frac{3}{4}$ in. plywood or hardwood. If hardwood is used make sure that the grain of the wood runs parallel to a line drawn from the centre of the base to the centre of the apex of the triangular shape of the spacer block. Trace from the template (Fig. 6) on to the wood and bore four $\frac{7}{8}$ in. diameter holes in the positions indicated. Stand the complete frame upright, and 'offer up' the blocks into position, marking the points at which the $\frac{1}{4}$ in. holes are to be drilled in the frame uprights. Make sure that the hole positions are in line with centres of the 'nut apertures' in the spacer

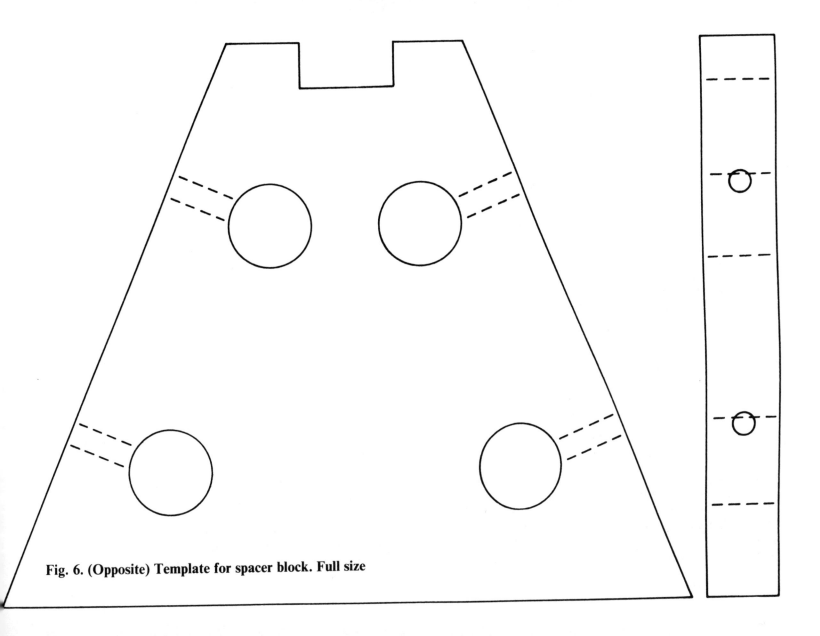

Fig. 6. (Opposite) Template for spacer block. Full size

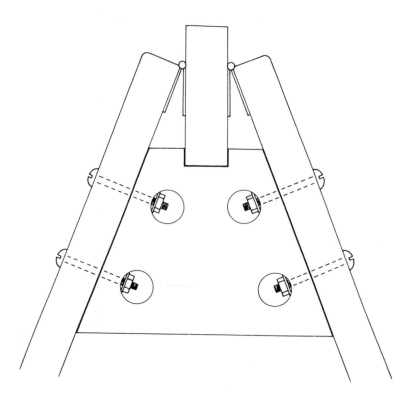

Fig. 7. Spacer block in position

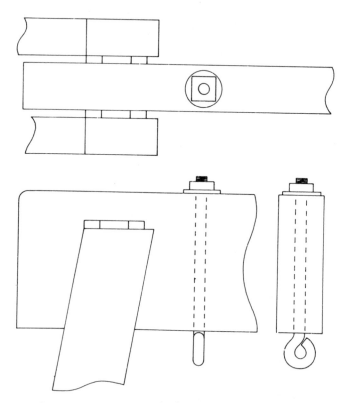

Fig. 8. Method of fixing eye-bolts in swing bar

blocks and at right-angles to the sides of the spacer blocks (Fig. 7). The holes in the uprights can be drilled and then used to mark the position of the bolt holes in the sides of the spacer blocks. The 2 in. bolts can be placed in position and the nuts and washers spun on to them in the 'nut apertures'. Tighten the bolts with the screwdriver, insert the eye-bolts in the swing bar

(Fig. 8), tighten the top bolts, and the frame is complete.

Should you wish to make the frame sturdier, a hole can be drilled centrally in the wider surface of each of the uprights 12 in. from the bottom, and a length of rope knotted from the front to the back upright to prevent the two U-shaped legs spreading outwards. Make sure that both the ropes are of the

172

same length and are securely knotted. They will not prevent the swing from folding flat when not in use and can therefore be left permanently in position.

The seat

The base of the swing seat is a 14 in. × 12 in. piece of $\frac{1}{2}$ in. plywood with the corners rounded off to an approximate radius of $\frac{1}{2}$ in. The slats forming the sides of the seat are 12 in. lengths of $\frac{7}{8}$ in. × $\frac{5}{8}$ in. timber; the front and back slats are 14 in. long. Cut four of each, round off the ends (the widest surface uppermost), and 1 in. from each end drill a $\frac{1}{4}$ in. hole centrally through the upper surface of each of the eight slats. The slats

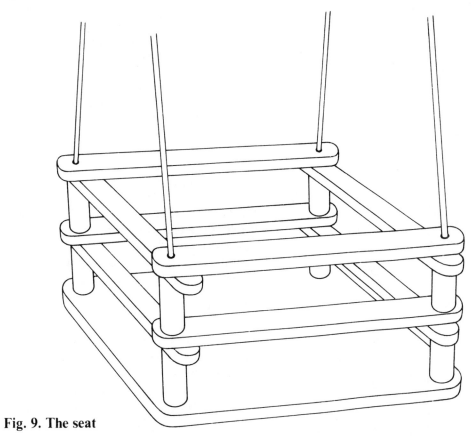

Fig. 9. The seat

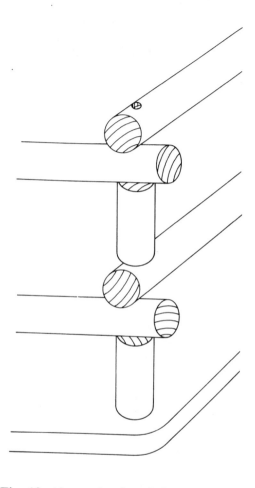

Fig. 10. Alternative dowel slats and spacers

can then be used to mark the corresponding holes in the corners of the seat base. Drill the four holes in the seat base, making sure that they line up perfectly with the slat holes or the support ropes will be chafed when the swing is moving to and fro. The slats can be of $\frac{7}{8}$ in. dowel if preferred (Fig. 10) but take great care to keep the holes aligned properly to prevent unnecessary chafing and strain of the support ropes. The dowel ends must be rounded off in the same way as the dowel spacers.

The spacers are 3 in. lengths of $\frac{7}{8}$ in. dowel with the upper and lower edges slightly rounded off (Fig. 11). A $\frac{1}{4}$ in. hole is drilled centrally through the length of each of the spacers and the whole unit is ready to thread together (Fig. 11). Wooden beads of 1 in. diameter (3 for each spacer) or $1\frac{1}{2}$ in. diameter (2 for each spacer) can be used instead of lengths of dowel if preferred (Fig. 12).

It is advisable to assemble the swing seat before painting to ensure that the holes in the slats and spacers line up correctly and that the slats are parallel to the seat base. Four knitting-needles or short lengths of string will do admirably to thread the parts together at this stage. Unbolt the two spacers from the frame, take the seat apart and sand smooth and paint all the separate pieces. Take great care not to fill the holes in any of the seat parts and make absolutely sure that all the parts are perfectly dry before final assembly.

The two support ropes are each a 100 in. length of Terylene/polyester or nylon rope. Each is firmly knotted at one end and then threaded through the front (the seat front and back are *across* the 14 in. width) holes in the seat base from underneath. The spacers and slats are threaded on the ropes in the order shown in Figs. 9 and 11. The last slat to be positioned is the top slat across the front of the swing. The ropes are then threaded through the top slat across the back of the seat and through the slats, the spacers and finally through the seat base

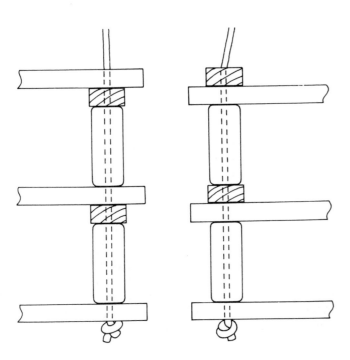

Fig. 11. Arrangement of slats and spacers

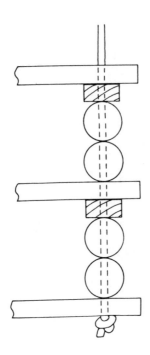

Fig. 12. Alternative use of wooden beads for spacers

175

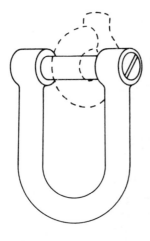

Fig. 13. Snap shackle

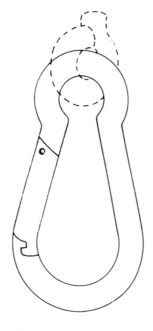

Fig. 14. Carbine hook

from above. The ends of the two ropes are securely knotted and the seat is lifted and checked to see that it hangs evenly and does not tilt to one side. The rope lengths are readily adjusted by undoing and slightly repositioning the knots. Make absolutely certain that the knots are secure and are large enough not to be drawn through the holes in the seat base.

The two side loops by which the swing is hung must now be looped either to snap shackles (Fig. 13) or to carbine hooks (Fig. 14), both of which are easily obtainable at most hardware and do-it-yourself stores.

It will be found easier to loop the support ropes to the shackles or hooks before fixing the shackles or hooks to the eye-bolts in the swing support bar. To ensure that the ropes do not slip and tip the child out of the swing the ropes must be securely knotted (Fig. 15a and b). To simplify tying the knot, loop the rope and slip it on to the shank of the hook or shackle.

The frame spacer blocks can now be bolted into position and

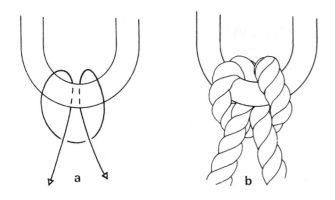

Fig. 15. Knot for support ropes: (a) diagrammatic, (b) actual

the hooks or shackles fitted to the eye-bolts. The baby-swing is now ready for use.

When the baby-swing is not required for play, remove the shackles or hooks (complete with seat) from the eye-bolts, unbolt the frame spacer blocks and fold the frame together. The complete swing can then easily be stored in a box-room, the garage or a garden shed.

MAINTENANCE

Check the support ropes at frequent intervals for signs of wear. The eye-bolts and frame should also be examined regularly to make sure that they are secure. Pay special attention to the frame joints.

See-saw

TOOLS

Tenon saw
Keyhole saw
Try square
Brace and bit (or drill) and countersink bit
$\frac{1}{4}$ in. and $\frac{3}{4}$ in. chisels and mallet
Pair of compasses
Rasp (half-round)
Sandpaper
Paintbrushes

MATERIALS AND METHOD

The see-saw (Fig. 1) is made from two basic structures: (a) the base and (b) the seat-board (Fig. 2). The base is made from $\frac{3}{4}$ in. plywood or blockboard with four lengths of 1 in. × 1 in. batten to strengthen the upright corners. The seat-board is a 60 in. length of $8\frac{1}{2}$ in. × $\frac{5}{8}$ in. timber with the spine board and handle uprights cut from $1\frac{7}{8}$ in. × $\frac{7}{8}$ in. softwood. The pivot bar is cut from a $10\frac{1}{2}$ in. length of $2\frac{1}{4}$ in. × $1\frac{7}{8}$ in. timber. This should preferably be of hardwood, but softwood will suffice if the see-saw is not misused by bigger children. The handles are simply 7 in. lengths of 1 in. diameter wooden dowel. The structures are glued and screwed together with $1\frac{1}{2}$ in.–$1\frac{3}{4}$ in. screws with the heads countersunk and the holes filled with cellulose filler or

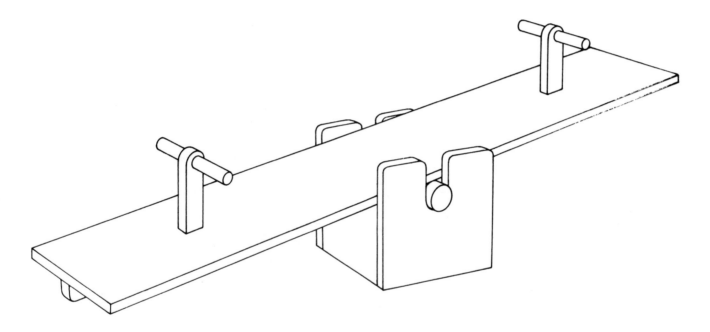

Fig. 1. The see-saw

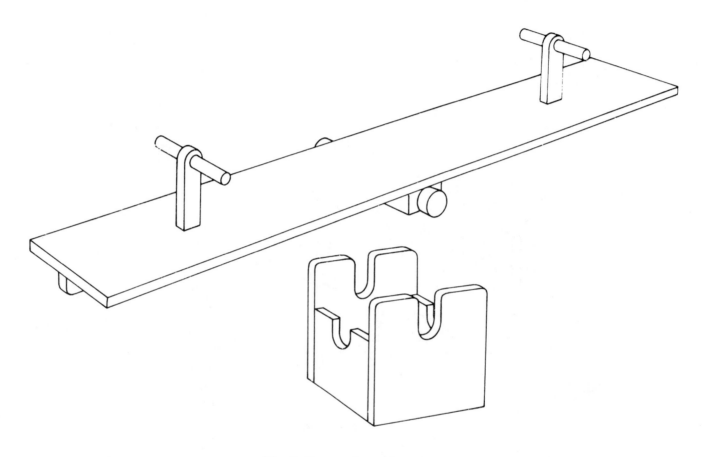

Fig. 2. Base and seat-board

plastic wood before finishing. The handles are glued and screwed or pinned into position in the handle uprights and the uprights are held in position with $\frac{3}{8}$ in. dowel 'pegs'.

The base

The base (Fig. 3) can be described as an open-topped box with two opposite sides taller than the other two. The seat-board pivots in slots on the two taller sides.

All four sides and the bottom of the base are cut from plywood or blockboard $\frac{3}{4}$ in. thick. The smaller ends are $8\frac{3}{4}$ in. × 10 in., the sides are $11\frac{1}{2}$ in. × 14 in. and the bottom of the 'box' is 10 in. × $8\frac{3}{4}$ in. The side panels upon which the seat-board pivots have centre slots $2\frac{3}{4}$ in. deep with a bottom radius of 1 in. The end panels have a centre slot $1\frac{1}{4}$ in. deep, also with a bottom radius of 1 in.

To make the U-shaped slots, first draw a line to divide the side and end panels widthways. On this line place the centre of a 2 in. diameter circle – $2\frac{3}{4}$ in. from the top of the side panels and 2 in. from the top of the end panels. Draw the circles completely. Then draw lines vertically to the top of the panels from the extreme width of the circles. *Make sure that the slots are parallel to the sides of the panels and of equal distance apart throughout their lengths.* The resulting 'U'-shape is then removed by drilling a line of holes round the *inside* of the bottom half of the circle, sawing down the inside of the vertical sides of the 'U' and removing the complete shape with either the mallet and chisel or a keyhole saw. The bottom curve of each pivot slot in particular must be smooth and as perfect a semicircle as possible. The slots in the base end-pieces are to allow sufficient clearance between the base and the spineboard when either end of the see-saw is in the 'down' position. The top corners of the side panels are now rounded off to the same radius as the 'U' slots.

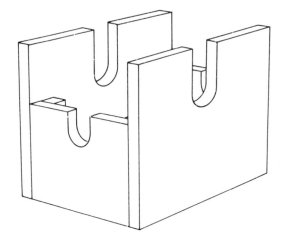

Fig. 3. Base

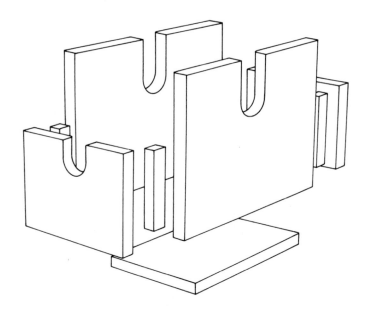

Fig. 4. Base: components

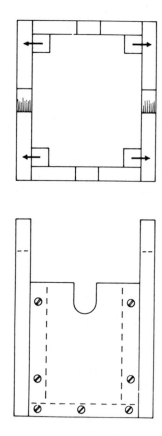

Fig. 5. Method of fixing battens inside base

The panels are glued and screwed together with strengthening battens at each corner (Figs. 4 and 5). The battens are 9 in. lengths of 1 in. square timber cut perfectly square and fixed to the *side* panels from the inside (Fig. 5). When the battens are glued and screwed in position ensure that a $\frac{3}{4}$ in. gap is left for the ends and bottom. The ends may now be glued and screwed in position. Check that the whole structure is square and firm. The bottom panel can now be fitted. *All screws must be countersunk and filled.*

The seat-board

The seat-board (Fig. 6) is a 60 in. length of $8\frac{1}{2}$ in. $\times$ $\frac{5}{8}$ in. timber. (If the see-saw is to be used by larger children it may be longer, but it *must* be thicker.) Two slots are cut in it to hold the handle uprights.

Mark a line along the centre of the upper surface of the board and 13 in. from each end mark a $1\frac{7}{8}$ in. rectangle. These rectangular areas must be carefully removed so that the $1\frac{7}{8}$ in. $\times$ $\frac{7}{8}$ in. handle uprights fit firmly within them without splitting the seat-board. To remove the waste, first drill a line of holes within the area to be removed and then chisel out the centre,

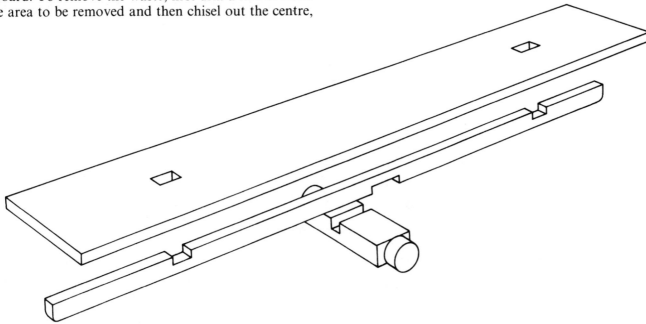

Fig. 6. Seat-board: components

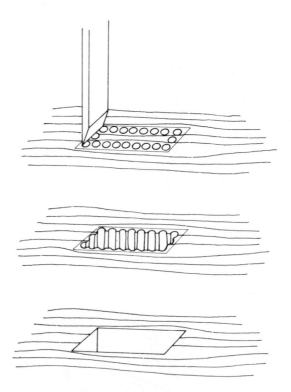

Fig. 7. Method of cutting slots in seat-board

taking care not to remove too much (Fig. 7). The rectangle is then carefully chiselled out, keeping the edges and corners square. Check that the $1\frac{7}{8}$ in. $\times \frac{7}{8}$ in. batten used for the handle uprights is a tight fit without having to be forced into the slots.

The spine-board is a 60 in. length of $1\frac{7}{8}$ in. $\times \frac{7}{8}$ in. timber with two slots $1\frac{7}{8}$ in. long by $\frac{7}{8}$ in. deep cut from the upper edge in the *exact positions* of the slots in the seat-board (Fig. 6). The female

parts of the 'T' joints formed by the handle uprights and the spine-boards are removed by first cutting the sides of the joint to a depth of $\frac{7}{8}$ in. and removing the waste with the mallet and chisel (Fig. 8). *Use the try square throughout to ensure that all corners and lines are square.* Check that the handlebar uprights fit firmly into the spine-board joints when inserted through the seat-board (Fig. 9).

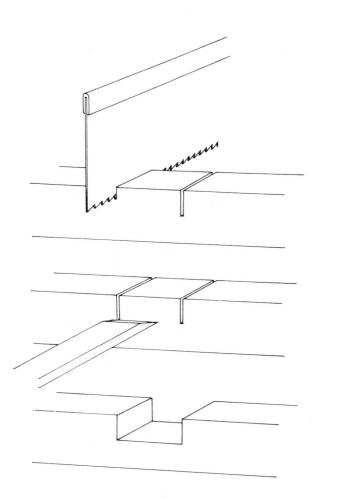

Fig. 8. Method of making 'T' joints in spine-board

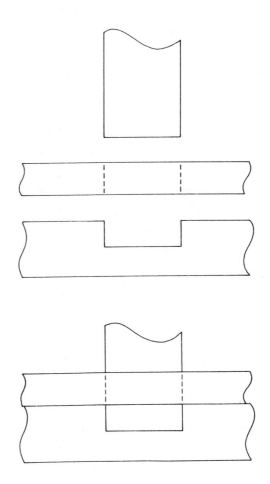

Fig. 9. Fitting handlebar uprights

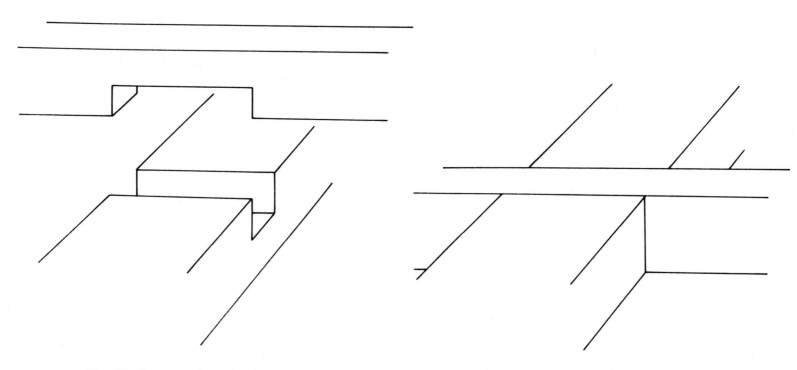

Fig. 10. Cross-halving joint for pivot bar

Fig. 11. Pivot bar in position

The pivot bar is a 10 in. length of $2\frac{1}{4}$ in. $\times$ $1\frac{7}{8}$ in. timber centrally 'cross-halved' with the spineboard and screwed to the underside of the seat-board (Figs. 6, 10 and 11). Centrally mark a cross-halving joint to a depth of $\frac{15}{16}$ in. on the underside of the spine-board and the upper surface (across the $2\frac{1}{4}$ in. surface) of the pivot bar and remove the waste in exactly the same way as the handle upright and spine-board 'T' joints (Fig. 8). Make sure that the cross-halving joint is firm and that the two pieces of timber are at right-angles to one another.

The spine-board can now be glued and screwed into position *centrally* along the length of the seat-board. Fix screws through the upper surface of the seat-board, countersinking and filling the holes. (If the see-saw is to be varnished you may prefer to fix the underside. Make sure that the screws do not protrude through the upper surface.) Round off the bottom corners of the spine-board.

The pivot bar must now be shaped to pivot in the slots of the sides of the see-saw base (Fig. 12). Using the try square mark a line round the pivot bar 1 in. from each end, leaving a $\frac{3}{4}$ in. gap in the centre of the two $2\frac{1}{4}$ in. surfaces. On each end of the pivot bar rule a diagonal line from corner to corner to find the *exact* centre on which to draw a $1\frac{7}{8}$ in. diameter circle with the compasses. Carefully cut with the tenon saw round the marked lines to a depth that will not remove any of the area within and between the two circles. With the chisel and mallet carefully remove most of the waste, making sure that the end circles are still intact. The rasp and sandpaper can now be used to finish the pivots. It is extremely important that the pivots are central and line up at each side; if they do not, the seat-board will rub and catch on the inner sides of the base. The pivot bar can now be glued and screwed into position. The handle uprights are simply two 9 in. lengths of $1\frac{7}{8}$ in. $\times$ $\frac{7}{8}$ in. timber rounded at the top end and drilled to take a 7 in. length of 1 in. diameter dowel

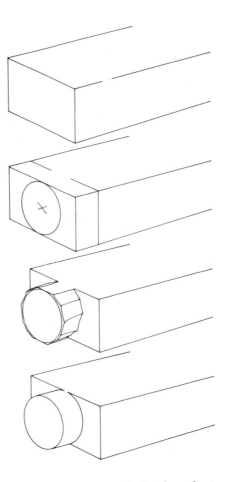

Fig. 12. Cutting and shaping pivots

which serves as the handlebars (Figs. 13 and 14). The holes to take the handles can easily be drilled by drawing a 1 in. diameter circle and drilling several holes within the area of the circle. The waste is then removed with a chisel and cleaned up with the rasp and sandpaper. Do *not* make the hole too large. It is easy to enlarge a hole but impossible to make it smaller. The dowel should be a tight fit and glued and screwed centrally into position. The screw-heads must be countersunk and filled. (If the see-saw is to be varnished, gluing and pinning should suffice.) Do not use screws that are too thick (they will split the dowel) or too short to enter the dowel, and 'stagger' them to avoid one screw fouling another.

The handle uprights can now be fitted into their slots and points marked for the holes to be drilled to take the $\frac{3}{8}$ in. dowel pegs. Make sure that the holes are drilled so that the pegs fit firmly and squarely against the underside of the seat-board (Fig. 15). The pegs must be a tight enough fit in the holes to have to be knocked in with the mallet.

The see-saw can now be painted or varnished and allowed to dry before placing the seat-board upon the base. The base can be filled with sand or even house-bricks to give the see-saw extra stability during play. Put whichever material you choose in a plastic bag and seal the opening before placing it in the base.

To pack the see-saw away when it is not in use the seat-board can be lifted off (and, if necessary, the dowel pegs knocked out and the handles removed). The whole structure is then of a size that can easily be stacked away.

The see-saw described here is for small children, but a larger version can easily be made. If the see-saw will be permanently outdoors, hardwood should be used; plywood or blockboard is *not* suitable. It is not necessary to make a 'box' base; the two side pieces can be embedded in the ground (or preferably in

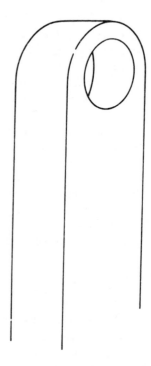

Fig. 13. Handle uprights

188

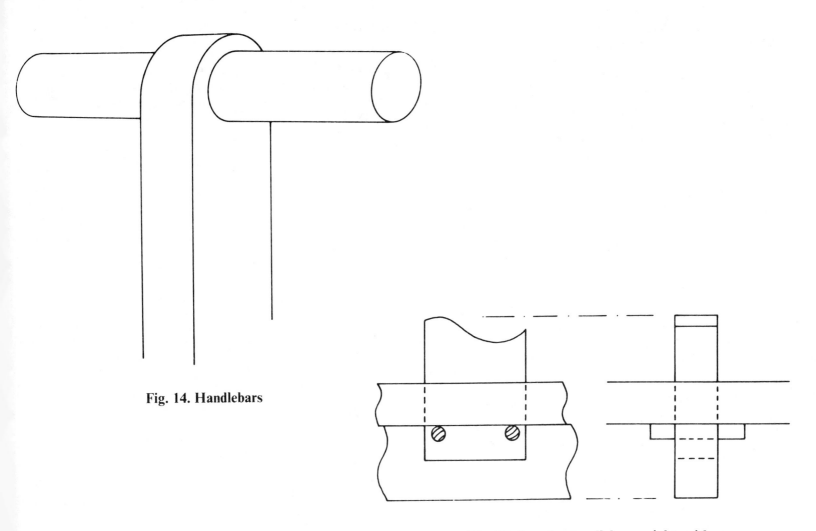

Fig. 14. Handlebars

Fig. 15. Securing handlebar uprights with pegs

concrete). The pivot height can be varied to suit the age and size of the children using the see-saw, but the sides of the base must be at least $1\frac{1}{2}$ in. thick and long enough for 16 in.–20 in. to be embedded. (Use creosote to protect this section.) The seat-board can be extended to 84 in. or even 90 in. long but it must be $\frac{7}{8}$ in.–1 in. thick. Do not use a wooden pivot bar for an outdoor see-saw: a length of mild steel tubing held in position by 'U'-bolts or saddle clips will do admirably.

MAINTENANCE

The see-saw should require very little attention, but it is wise to inspect it at frequent intervals. Make sure that the base is firm and that the spine-board, pivot bar and handles are secure. At the same time, check that there are no splinters that could cause injury.

Toddler's scooter

Fig. 1. The scooter

TOOLS

Tenon saw
Try square or set square
Fretsaw or coping saw
Brace and bit or drill and countersink bit
Chisel ($\frac{1}{2}$ in.) and mallet
Pair of compasses or jar or tin lid with diameter of 5 in.
Hacksaw
Flat file
Sandpaper
Paintbrushes

MATERIALS

The toddler's scooter (Fig. 1) is made almost entirely from $\frac{3}{4}$ in. and 1 in. timber and plywood. The steering upright and the foot platform are of $3\frac{3}{4}$ in. $\times$ $\frac{3}{4}$ in. timber (or $3\frac{3}{4}$ in. $\times$ 1 in. timber may be used to make an even sturdier frame). The wheels are of 1 in. plywood or of several thicknesses of thinner plywood glued together. The steering pivot is cut from timber $\frac{7}{8}$ in. thick. The handlebar is a length of $1\frac{1}{4}$ in. $\times$ $\frac{7}{8}$ in. wood; or if 1 in. timber is used for the steering upright the handlebar must be $\frac{1}{8}$ in. thicker than the upright, i.e. $1\frac{1}{8}$ in. The back axle support is of the same thickness, but $1\frac{3}{4}$ in. wide. The axles are of $\frac{1}{2}$ in. diameter wooden dowel; but note that $\frac{3}{8}$ in. dowel must be used

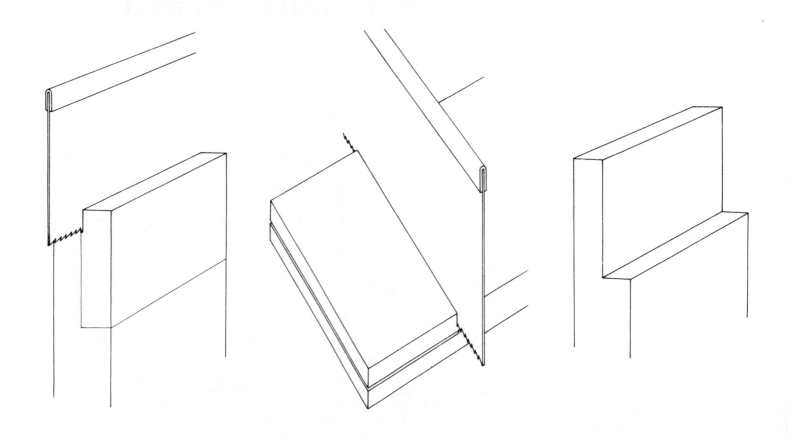

Fig. 2. Cutting halving joint: upright

for the front wheel if $\frac{3}{4}$ in. timber is used for the upright. The wheel washers are of thin plywood, linoleum or any other suitable material $\frac{1}{8}$ in. thick. The swivel pin is a $3\frac{5}{8}$ in. length of mild steel rod; or a 4 in. nail can be used. The main frame of the scooter is made of two lengths of $3\frac{3}{4}$ in. × $\frac{3}{4}$ in. timber, the upright section being 19 in. long and the foot platform 14 in. *N.B. All dimensions are finished sizes: allow extra for waste and finishing.*

METHOD

The handlebar is held in position by a 'T' halving joint (Fig. 2). The top edge of the upright is marked centrally across the width and sawn to a depth of $1\frac{1}{4}$ in. (Fig. 2a). Cut on the waste side of the marked line (Fig. 2b). The shoulders and corners must be square (Fig. 2c). The handlebar is a 10 in. length of wood $1\frac{1}{4}$ in. wide and $\frac{1}{8}$ in. thicker than the upright. The width of the upright is marked centrally across the handlebar section and two saw-cuts made to the same depth as the divided section of the upright (Fig. 3a). Once again cut on the waste side of the marked lines. The centre section is then removed with the chisel and mallet (Fig. 3b). It may be found easier to remove the waste if several saw-cuts are made between the first two – but be careful not to cut below the depth of the two outermost saw-cuts. Once again check that the shoulders are square (Fig. 3c). Then check that the two parts of the joint fit tightly and squarely together.

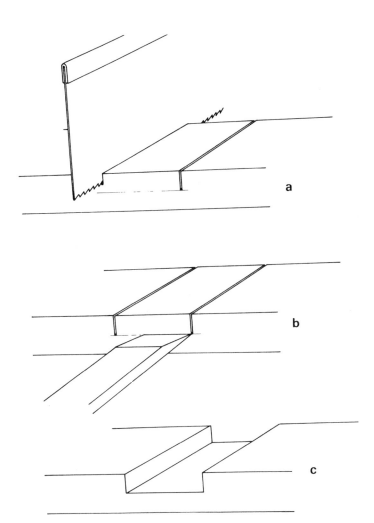

Fig. 3. Cutting halving joint: handlebar

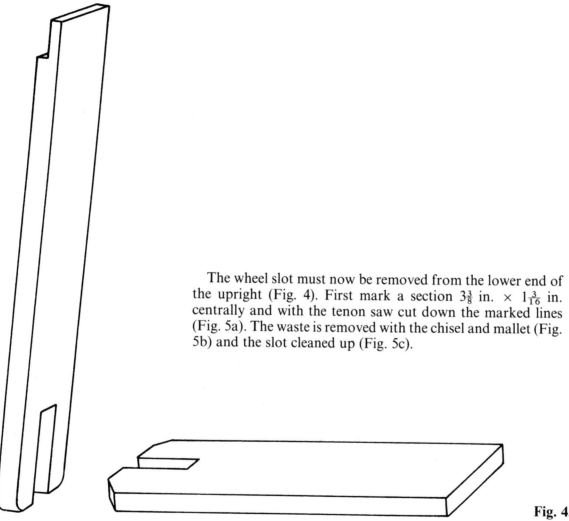

The wheel slot must now be removed from the lower end of the upright (Fig. 4). First mark a section $3\frac{3}{8}$ in. $\times$ $1\frac{3}{16}$ in. centrally and with the tenon saw cut down the marked lines (Fig. 5a). The waste is removed with the chisel and mallet (Fig. 5b) and the slot cleaned up (Fig. 5c).

Fig. 4. Upright and foot platform

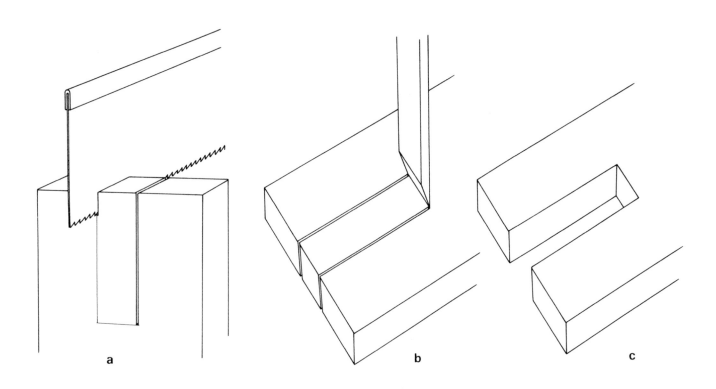

Fig. 5. Cutting wheel slot

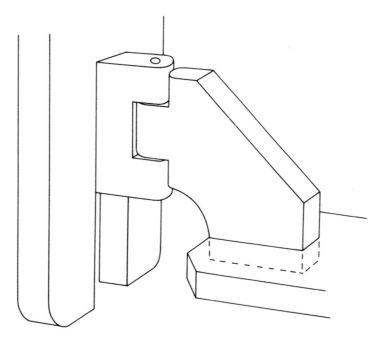

Fig. 6. Steering pivot

The bottom outer corners may now be rounded off and the axle holes drilled through each fork (Fig. 15 shows the correct position). If the upright is $\frac{3}{4}$ in. thick, a $\frac{3}{8}$ in. diameter hole is the largest that can be drilled to take a wooden axle. A hole of smaller diameter using a length of nail with a wooden plug at each outer end, made in the same way as the steering swivel pin (see Fig. 10), will do admirably. If timber 1 in. thick is used for the upright, $\frac{1}{2}$ in. dowel can be used for the axle. Ensure that the holes in each fork line up correctly and that the axle is a tight enough fit to have to be knocked into position with the mallet. Do *not* at this stage fit the axle, or you will not be able to fit the wheel and washers.

The foot platform has the slot cut from the leading end in exactly the same way as the front fork (see Fig. 4). The width of

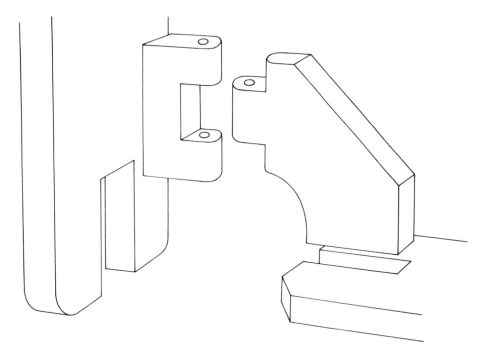

Fig. 7. Steering pivot: components

the slot is exactly the same as the thickness of the steering pivot parts (see Fig. 6). The back axle support is simply a $3\frac{3}{4}$ in. length of $1\frac{3}{4}$ in. $\times$ $\frac{7}{8}$ in. timber drilled through almost at the upper edge to take the $\frac{1}{2}$ in. diameter axle, then screwed to the underside of the platform $\frac{3}{4}$ in. from the rear end (see Fig. 14). If difficulty is experienced in drilling so close to the upper surface of the axle support, a slot can be cut with the bottom rounded off. To do this, wrap a piece of sandpaper round the axle dowel and sand in a to and fro motion. The underside of the foot platform can have a slight indentation, not more than $\frac{1}{16}$ in. deep, sanded in the same way, enabling the dowel to rotate as if in a circular hole. Make sure that the axle rotates freely with virtually no horizontal or vertical movement.

The steering pivot (Figs. 6 and 7) is made from two parts

197

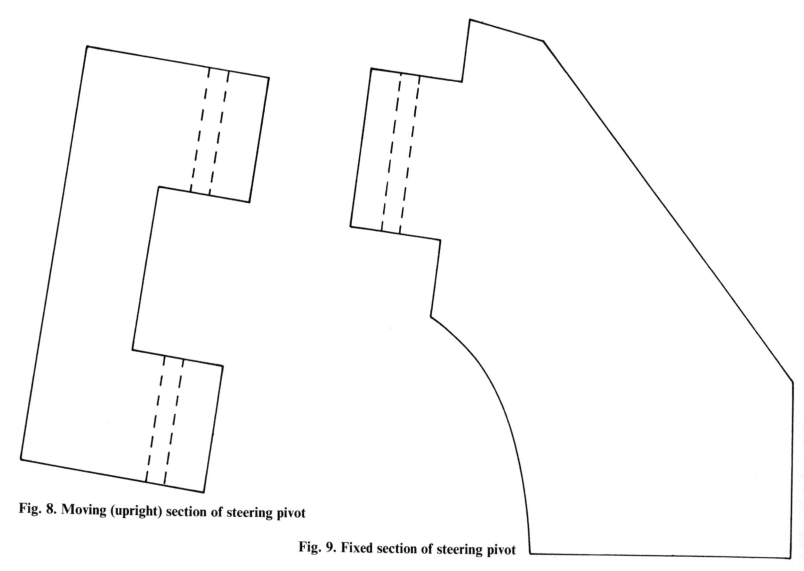

Fig. 8. Moving (upright) section of steering pivot

Fig. 9. Fixed section of steering pivot

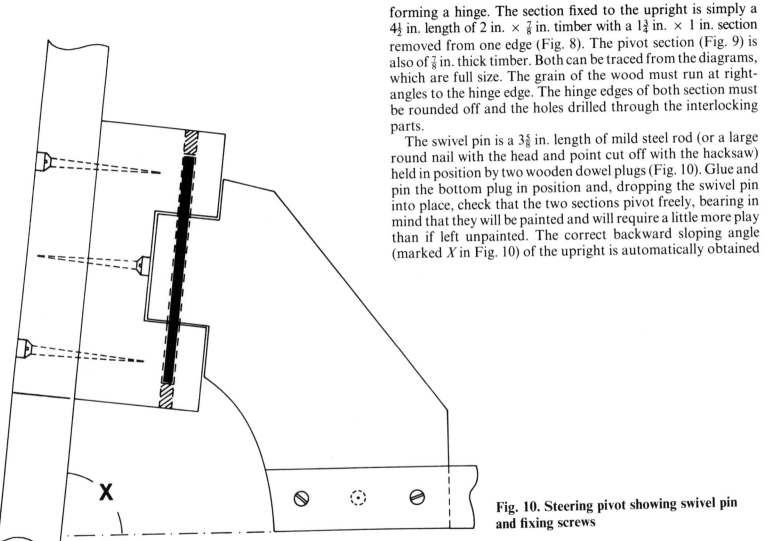

forming a hinge. The section fixed to the upright is simply a $4\frac{1}{2}$ in. length of 2 in. $\times$ $\frac{7}{8}$ in. timber with a $1\frac{3}{4}$ in. $\times$ 1 in. section removed from one edge (Fig. 8). The pivot section (Fig. 9) is also of $\frac{7}{8}$ in. thick timber. Both can be traced from the diagrams, which are full size. The grain of the wood must run at right-angles to the hinge edge. The hinge edges of both section must be rounded off and the holes drilled through the interlocking parts.

The swivel pin is a $3\frac{5}{8}$ in. length of mild steel rod (or a large round nail with the head and point cut off with the hacksaw) held in position by two wooden dowel plugs (Fig. 10). Glue and pin the bottom plug in position and, dropping the swivel pin into place, check that the two sections pivot freely, bearing in mind that they will be painted and will require a little more play than if left unpainted. The correct backward sloping angle (marked X in Fig. 10) of the upright is automatically obtained

Fig. 10. Steering pivot showing swivel pin and fixing screws

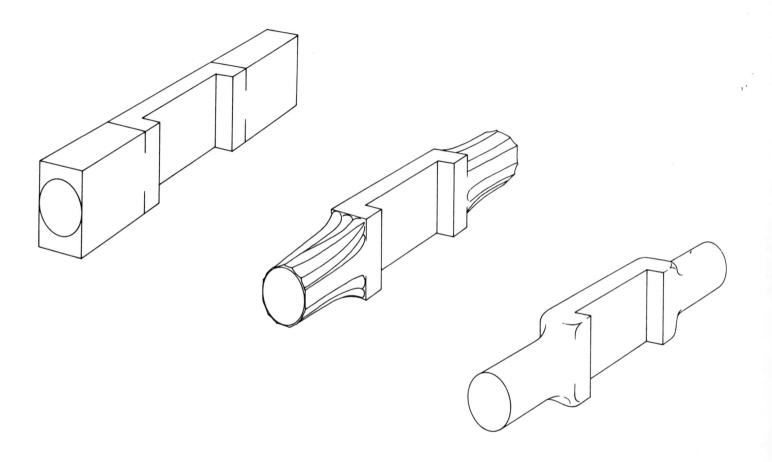

Fig. 11. Shaping the handlebars

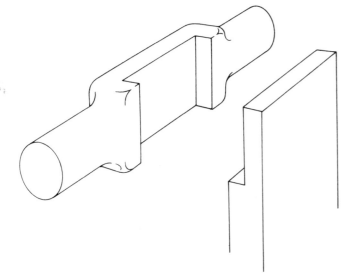

Fig. 12. Handlebar joint

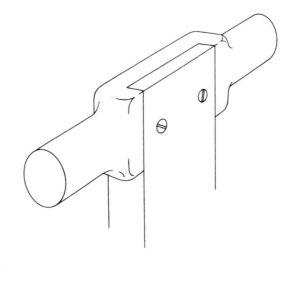

Fig. 13. Handlebar fitted to upright

when the steering pivot is correctly assembled. Remove the swivel pin and glue and screw the upright section to the steering upright and the swivel section into the slot of the foot platform. The screws must be positioned as shown in Fig. 10 and must be countersunk and filled. Do *not* at this point assemble the two parts.

The handlebar can now be shaped and fitted to the steering upright. Mark a point at the centre of each end of the bar and with the compasses scribe a circle of diameter equal to the

thickness of the bar. Mark a line round the upper and lower thirds of the bar, $\frac{1}{2}$ in. from the ends of the shoulders of the removed section (Fig. 11a). With the chisel carefully remove the waste from the shoulder lines, taking care not to remove any of the end circles (Fig. 11b). The handlebars can now be properly shaped and sanded (Fig. 11c). Strips of sandpaper glued to pieces of card make excellent files for shaping. The finished handlebar may now be glued and screwed to the upright (Figs. 12 and 13). Place the screws in positions similar

201

to those in the steering swivel, one from the front and two from the rear, making sure that each screw-head is countersunk and filled (see Fig. 10).

The wheels are now cut from 1 in. plywood (or several thicknesses of thinner ply glued together to make 1 in.). With the compasses scribe three 5 in. diameter circles. Cut them out carefully with the fretsaw or coping saw and sand them smooth, rounding off the edges. Hints on using a fretsaw are given on p. 8. The front wheel spins on its axle and its central hole must be large enough to allow it to turn freely. The back wheels are fixed to the axle, which rotates in the axle support; so the holes in the centre of the wheels must be a tight enough fit for them to have to be hammered home. *Do not fit the wheels yet.*

Four large washers are needed to enable the wheels to rotate without rubbing or catching the scooter (Figs. 14–16). These are $1\frac{1}{8}$ in. in diameter and must also spin freely on the axles.

The scooter can now be painted or varnished to your choice. Allow it at least 48 hours to dry. If the scooter parts are assembled before the paint or vanish has dried properly, the pivoted sections will stick or become damaged.

The front wheel is fitted by inserting the axle through one fork, through one washer, the wheel, another washer and into the other fork (Fig. 15). If the axle is cut to the exact width of the upright and sanded smooth at each end before fitting, there will be no risk of damaging the forks by trying to cut and sand the axle ends off flush after fitting. If panel pins are used to secure the axle, do not forget a touch of paint on the heads when you paint the axle ends.

The back axle can also be cut to length before fitting and then glued and hammered home into one wheel before inserting it into the axle support. Slip a washer over the axle, insert the axle through the axle support and fit another washer before gluing

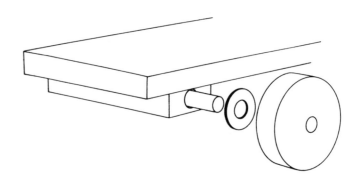

Fig. 14. Rear wheel, axle and washer

the other wheel into position (Fig. 16). The axles can be made to fit even tighter if the ends are split before gluing, and wedges glued and hammered into the splits.

The two steering pivots can now be mated and the swivel pin inserted. Cut the top plug square and smooth it off before gluing it into position so that all that is needed to hide it is a touch of paint or varnish. The scooter is now ready.

Should you wish to make a larger scooter, the steering upright and foot platform have only to be extended by a couple of inches. A scooter for a much older child must have a stronger pivot and metal axles. Metal or plastic wheels are cheap and easily obtainable. These instructions can also be adapted for a smaller scooter or one with only two wheels.

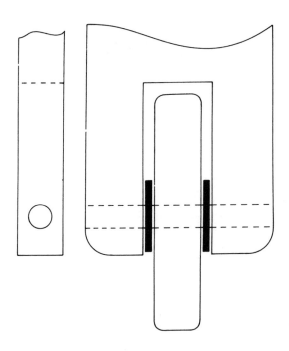

Fig. 15. Front wheel and axle assembled

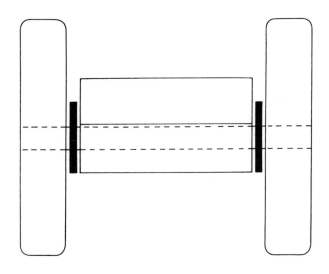

Fig. 16. Rear wheel and axle assembled

MAINTENANCE

The scooter should require little attention, but a regular check is a wise precaution. Make sure that all the joints are secure and check that the steering pivot is in good order. At the same time look out for any splinters that might cause injury.

Toddler's tricycle

TOOLS

Tenon saw
Try square or set square
Block plane or smoothing plane
Brace and bit or drill, and countersink bit
$\frac{1}{2}$ in. chisel and mallet
Pair of compasses
Rasp
Sandpaper
Paintbrushes
Hacksaw
Flat file
$\frac{1}{4}$ in. metal drill

MATERIALS

With the exception of the steering bracket and bolt and the pedal bolts, the entire tricycle (Fig. 1) is cut from plywood and timber. The seat and wheels are cut from $\frac{3}{4}$ in. plywood, the main 'T' frame is cut from $1\frac{3}{4}$ in. square timber, and the handlebar pillar from $1\frac{3}{4} \times 2\frac{3}{4}$ in. timber. The cranks and the front and rear forks are of $\frac{3}{8}$ in. plywood, and $\frac{3}{4}$ in. timber is used for the pedals. The rear axle is of 1 in. dowel.

This toy can be made without pedals as a 'push-along' tricycle.

Fig. 1. The tricycle

When the tricycle is built according to these instructions, the handlebars will be 22 in. from the ground and the seat 14 in. from the ground. Should you wish to reduce the size, the forks can be shortened as necessary. In this case, note that the front wheel diameter must be reduced by half the amount by which the front fork is shortened, and the cranks shortened also.

METHOD

Main frame and forks

The 'T' section of the main frame is made from two 13 in. lengths of $1\frac{3}{4}$ in. square timber (Fig. 2). The longitudinal bar which slots into the bracket on the handlebar pillar is $9\frac{1}{2}$ in. long. This includes the $\frac{3}{4}$ in. which forms the male part of the 'T' joint. The bar which supports the seat and rear fork is 7 in. long. The angles of the seat support will be correct if a line is drawn $\frac{1}{2}$ in. from each end of the upper surface and saw-cuts are made to the bottom extreme ends (Fig. 3). Make sure that the ends of the upper surface are perfectly square; use your try square at all times.

The longitudinal bar sides are rounded at the bracket end

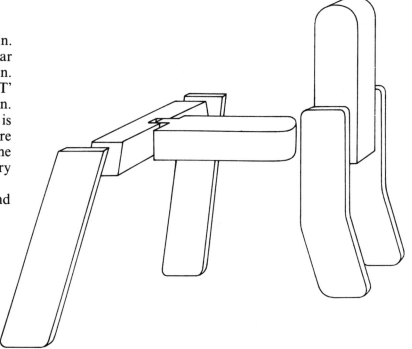

Fig. 2. Tricycle frame: components

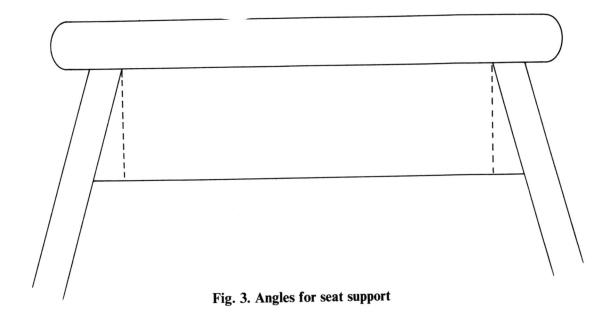

Fig. 3. Angles for seat support

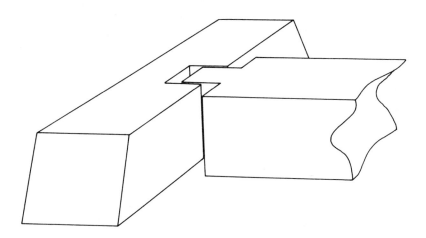

Fig. 4. 'T' joint for frame

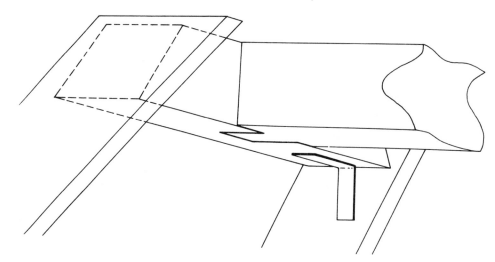

Fig. 5. Angle brackets fitted to 'T' joint

and a $\frac{1}{4}$ in. hole is drilled right through the bar centrally from the upper surface, 1 in. from the end (Fig. 9).

The two bars are simply glued together at the 'T' joint (Fig. 4). Angle brackets or a 'T' bracket can be used if desired (Fig. 5), but in any case the joint is further strengthened when the seat is fixed in position.

The handlebar pillar is an $8\frac{1}{2}$ in. length of $2\frac{3}{4}$ in. $\times$ $1\frac{3}{4}$ in. timber, rounded at the top end and drilled to take the 10 in. length of 1 in. diameter dowel which serves as the handlebars (Fig. 6). The hole to take the handlebars can easily be drilled by scribing a 1 in. diameter circle and drilling several holes within this area. The waste can then be removed with a chisel. Do *not* make the hole too large. The dowel must be a tight fit and should be glued and screwed into position as illustrated. The screw heads must be countersunk and filled with plastic wood or filler. Do not use screws that are too thick, or they will split the dowel. Nor must they be too short to enter the dowel. Stagger them to prevent one screw from fouling another.

The forks are cut from $\frac{3}{8}$ in. plywood although, if extra strength is required, $\frac{1}{2}$ in. plywood may be used. But if you use thicker plywood remember to allow for the extra thickness when cutting the axles.

The rear fork is made from two pieces, each 13 in. $\times$ $2\frac{1}{2}$ in. The angle at the top, which slopes the fork backwards, is arrived at by marking a point $\frac{3}{4}$ in. from the top at the back edge and ruling a line from that point to the top front corner (Fig. 7). This means that the top edge will fit tightly beneath the seat, as shown in Fig. 5.

The bottom ends of the fork may be rounded, or only the corners rounded off.

Holes must now be drilled to take the back axle. They must be 11 in. from the top. Measure centrally down the length of the fork.

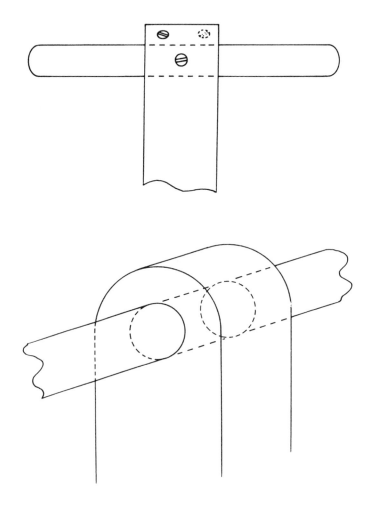

Fig. 6. Handlebar mounting

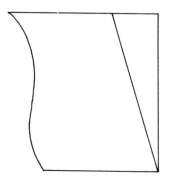

Fig. 7. Setting out angles for rear forks

The two lengths of fork must now be fixed to the ends of the seat support. A wood glue may be used with two $1\frac{1}{2}$ in. screws, but be careful not to split the ends of the seat bar. Two angle brackets may be used to strengthen the joint (see Fig. 4) and a short bolt through the fork legs used instead of a screw. Further strength is given to the back fork by the back axle, which is fixed and does not rotate.

An 18 in. length of 1 in. dowel is glued and pinned through the two fork axle holes so that an equal length of dowel protrudes at each end.

The front fork is also cut from $\frac{3}{8}$ in. plywood, each leg being shaped from a section measuring 4 in. × 11 in. The fork 'bends' forward (see Figs. 1 and 2). This shape is made by first ruling a line 3 in. from the back edge of the piece of plywood to a point 6 in. from the top edge. From the bottom of the 6 in. line draw a line to the front bottom corner. You now have a 'bent' line which is the front edge of the fork leg. Rule another line parallel to and 3 in. from the bottom part of the bent line and you have the complete shape. Cut out, then round off the corners.

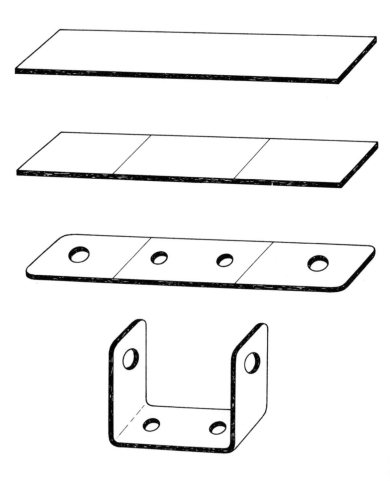

Fig. 8. Making the steering bracket

210

The holes for the front axle must be 1 in. in diameter and 1 in. from the bottom of the legs. This, of course, means that the centre of the hole is $1\frac{1}{2}$ in. from the bottom of the fork legs. *Do not fix the front fork to the handlebar pillar at this stage.*

The steering bracket

Mark the steel bar $1\frac{1}{2}$ in. from each end and drill two holes within the area marked to take the screws to attach the bracket to the handlebar pillar (Fig. 8). Two larger holes must now be drilled, not more than $\frac{1}{2}$ in. from each end of the steel bar, to take the steering bolt. The bar should then be bent into a 'U' shape, keeping the corners as sharp and as square as possible. Make sure that the steering bolt slips into both holes in a line parallel to the centre section of the bracket, as well as perpendicularly, one above the other. File all edges and corners smooth and fix the 'T' bar and steering bar together (Fig. 9). Make sure the handlebar pillar swivels easily.

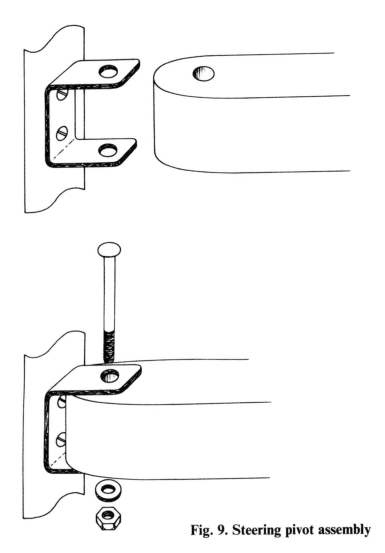

Fig. 9. Steering pivot assembly

211

A stronger and longer-lasting steering pivot can be made by simply adding two metal plates, as shown in Fig. 10. If this method is used, make sure that the steering bolt rotates freely in the holes of the metal plates.

The wheels

The wheels are cut from $\frac{3}{4}$ in. plywood. The two back wheels are 6 in. in diameter, the front wheel 12 in. The back wheels are marked out with a pair of compasses and then cut out with a narrow-bladed saw. Before cutting round the circle, first drill the axle hole, making absolutely sure that it is positioned centrally in the circle. Then cut out the wheel and smooth the edges. Check continually that the axle hole is central, or someone is going to have a bumpy ride. Check also that the wheels slide easily over the back axle.

The front wheel contains its own axle upon which the pedal arms must be fixed, and it is thus not quite so simple to make.

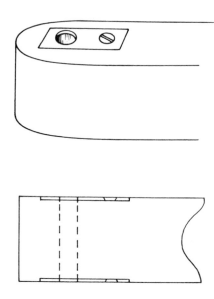

Fig. 10. Steering pivot reinforced with steel plate

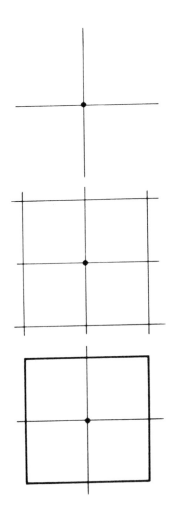

Fig. 11. Marking out the hole in wheel

First draw the 12 in. circle, clearly marking the centre. Rule a line across the centre point and, at right-angles to that line, draw another line so that it crosses the centre (Fig. 11).

Next, mark out a $1\frac{3}{4}$ in. square by measuring and marking a point $\frac{7}{8}$ in. along each line from the centre. It will now be found simple to mark out the $1\frac{3}{4}$ in. square, which must be completely removed with the chisel and mallet. The $1\frac{3}{4}$ in. square block from which the axle is cut must be an extremely tight fit, so be careful not to remove too much. The wheel can now be cut out and sanded smooth. Take care not to alter the shape or the axle hole will no longer be central.

The front axle is easily made from a 4 in. length of $1\frac{3}{4}$ in.

square timber (Fig. 12a). Using a try square, mark a line round the axle bar, $1\frac{1}{2}$ in. from each end. On each end of the axle bar, rule a diagonal line from corner to corner to find the exact centre upon which to draw a 1 in. circle with the compasses (Fig. 12b). Using the tenon saw, carefully cut round the marked lines to a depth of $\frac{1}{4}$ in., cutting slightly deeper at the corners (Fig. 12c). With a chisel and mallet, carefully remove most of the waste, making sure that the end circles are not cut into (Fig. 12d).

The rasp and sandpaper can now be used to finish the axle (Fig. 12e). It is extremely important that the round hubs are central and line up at each side.

The hub can now be glued centrally into the wheel. Make sure that it is a really tight fit, in fact so tight that it has to be knocked in with a mallet.

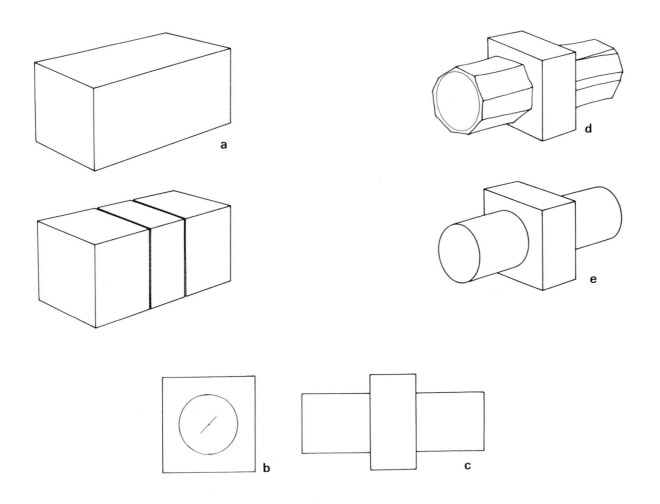

Fig. 12. Shaping front axle

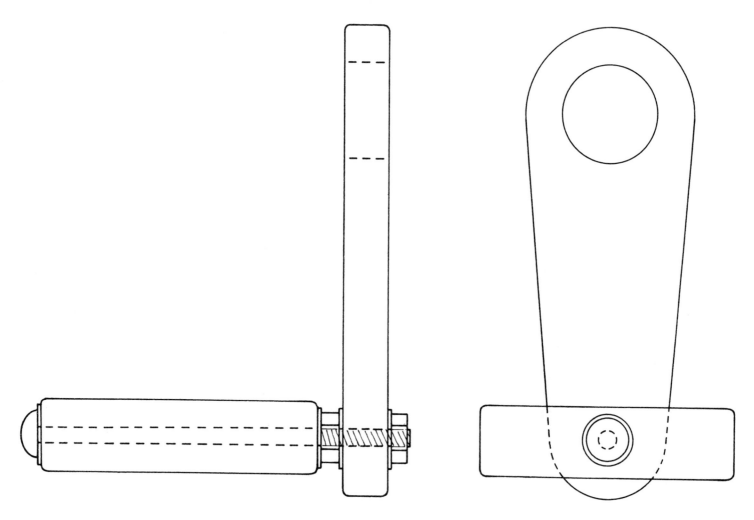

Fig. 13. Pedals and cranks

The pedals

The cranks are cut from pieces of $\frac{3}{8}$ in. plywood 5 in. long, tapering from $1\frac{7}{8}$ to $1\frac{1}{4}$ in. (Fig. 13). Centrally mark a point $\frac{15}{16}$ in. from the top of the crank as the centre of the axle hole and the top semicircular curve. With the compasses, scribe the $\frac{15}{16}$ in. arc and the 1 in. axle hole. The axle hole must be a very tight fit on the front axle; so be careful not to cut it too large.

Centrally mark a point $\frac{7}{8}$ in. from the bottom of the crank and scribe a $\frac{7}{8}$ in. arc. Use the centre of the arc as the point to drill the hole to hold the pedal bolt. Sand smooth and round off all edges.

The pedal is a block of timber $2\frac{3}{4}$ in. $\times$ 3 in. $\times$ $\frac{3}{4}$ in., drilled through centrally to take the 4 in. bolt. Round off all edges and attach it to the crank using four washers and two bolts as illustrated in Fig. 13.

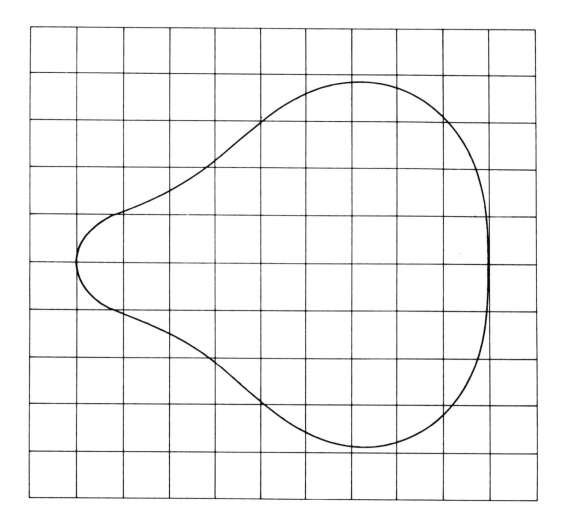

Fig. 14. Seat

The seat

Use the grid marked on the seat plan to cut the seat to shape. The grid in Fig. 14 represents 1 in. squares. Draw your own grid of 1 in. squares and transfer the shape by marking with dots on your grid each point where the lines of the seat shape illustrated cross the lines of the grid in Fig. 14. Join up the dots, taking care to follow the shape of the curves shown. Your plan will now be full size.

Should you find difficulty in cutting the shape with the narrow-bladed saw, drill holes round the shape and cut as illustrated.

Sand the seat smooth and fix it in position on the seat bar and main bar of the tricycle frame (Fig. 15). *The screw heads must be countersunk and filled.*

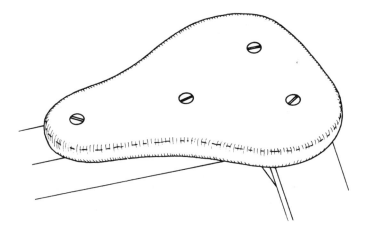

Fig. 15. Seat screwed in position

219

Finishing and assembling

All the parts can now be painted in your choice of colours, and assembled when completely dry.

Glue and screw the front fork leg on one side, using three $1\frac{1}{4}$ in dome-headed screws. Place a $\frac{3}{8}$ in. thick washer over one axle of the front wheel and insert the axle into the hole on the fixed fork leg. (You can cut the washers from plywood or a material such as linoleum.)

Place another $\frac{3}{8}$ in. washer over the other side of the axle and position the other fork leg over it. Before gluing and fixing the leg into position, make sure that the wheel spins freely and does not touch the inside of either fork or the bottom of the handlebar pillar.

The cranks and pedals are now bolted together. Ensure that the pedal spins freely on the pedal bolt. Place a spacer washer $\frac{1}{2}$ in. thick, made in the same way as the wheel washers, on the protruding axle, and then glue and pin the crank into position. *Make sure that the protruding nut holding the pedal to the pedal arm does not touch the fork.*

The procedure is exactly the same for the other side, with the pedals lining up on opposite sides of the wheel, so that when one pedal is up the other is down. Make sure that there is enough play between each of the fork arms and washers, wheel and washers, and between the cranks and washers, and that the wheels and pedals spin freely.

Wedge-shaped washers need to be fixed in position to enable the wheels to run freely and upright. The wedge is a slice from the $1\frac{3}{4}$ in. square timber used for the main frame, with a 1 in. hole drilled through. Fig. 17 shows how the angle is the same as that of the seat bar ends. The wedge is glued and pinned into position on the rear fork leg and a $\frac{1}{4}$ in. washer placed on the protruding axle. The wheel is then placed over the axle and

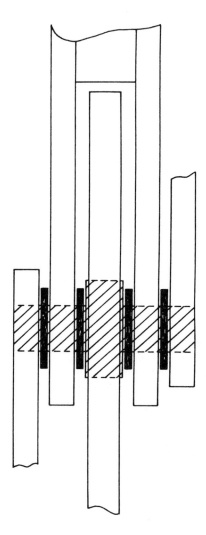

Fig. 16. Front axle assembly

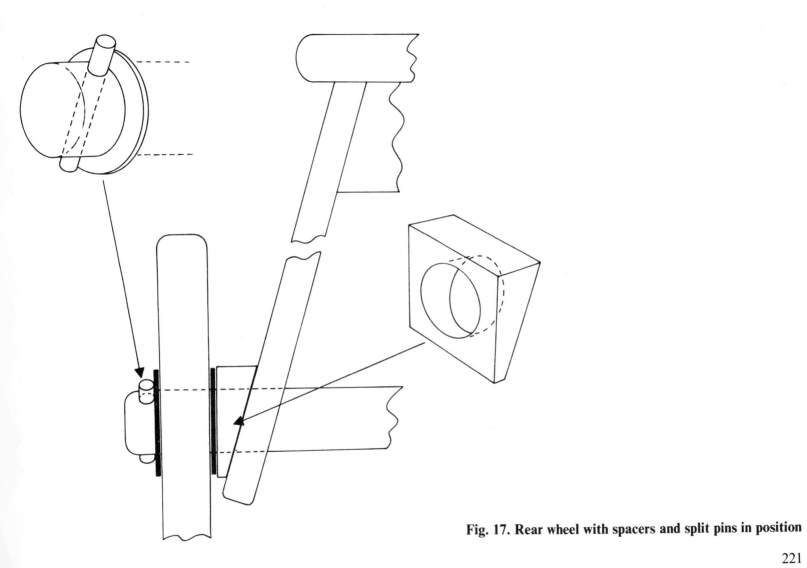

Fig. 17. Rear wheel with spacers and split pins in position

another $\frac{1}{4}$ in. washer on top. A $\frac{1}{4}$ in. hole is then drilled through the axle and a $1\frac{1}{4}$ in. length of dowel glued into position as shown in Fig. 17.

Repeat the operation for the other side, and the tricycle is ready.

MAINTENANCE

The tricycle should require little attention, but a regular check is a wise precaution. Make sure that all joints are secure and that the steering pivot is in good order. Look at the same time for any splinters that might cause injury.